LEGENDS OF NASCAR

TRIUMPH
B O O K S
CHICAGO

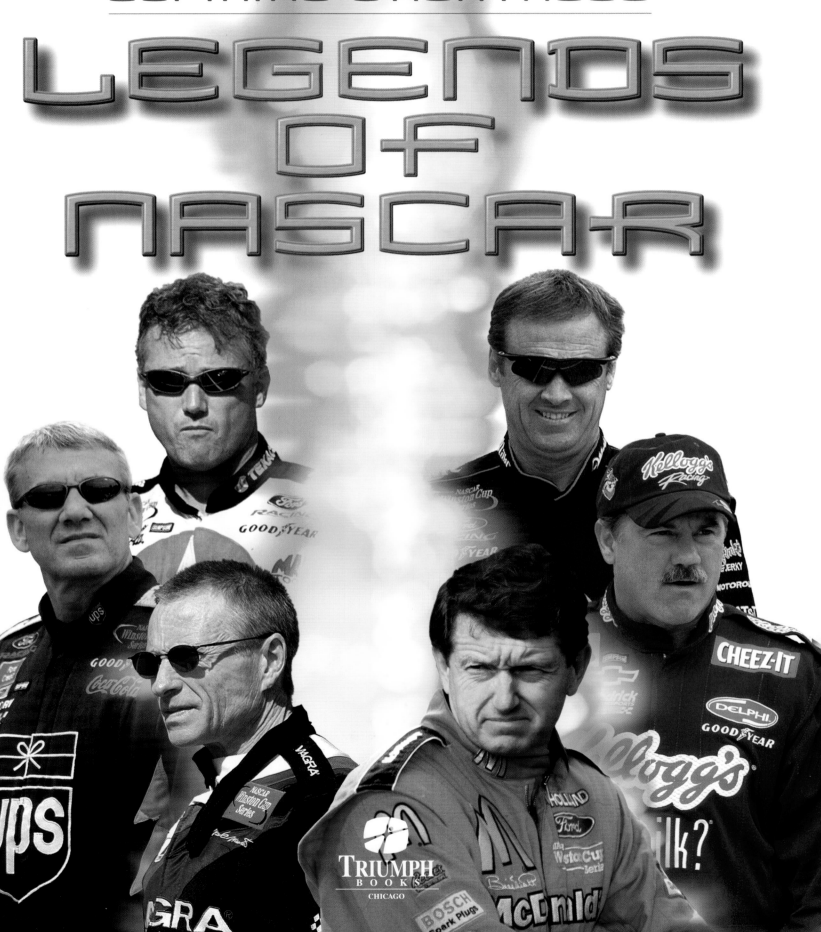

DEFYING TIME...
DEFINING GREATNESS

LEGENDS
OF
NASCAR

TRIUMPH
BOOKS
CHICAGO

Authors:

Woody Cain is a journalist living in Concord, North Carolina, with his wife, Sandy. A graduate of Appalachian State University, he has covered motorsports for radio, television, and print since 1987. Cain is host of the live call-in television program *Let's Talk Racing*, and play-by-play announcer for the televised *Around the Track* racing productions and specials.

Other professional credits include work as a general reporter and editor for daily, weekly, and monthly publications, as well as radio news/sports director at WEGO-AM in Concord and WABZ-FM in Albemarle, North Carolina. Cain currently works as editor of *The Charlotte Observer's University City Magazine* in Charlotte, North Carolina.

Jason Mitchell is a veteran NASCAR Winston Cup Series freelance writer who resides in Concord, North Carolina.

Mitchell was born August 14, 1972, in Fort Walton Beach, Florida. While he was young, Mitchell's family moved to North Wilkesboro, North Carolina. His love for auto racing began while growing up around the now-defunct North Wilkesboro Speedway, which until 1996 hosted two NASCAR Winston Cup Series races a year.

Mitchell graduated from Appalachian State University in Boone, North Carolina, in 1996 with a bachelor of science degree in communications. He majored in public relations with a minor in marketing.

Upon graduation, Mitchell became assistant sports editor at the *Wilkes Journal-Patriot*. Trying to get closer to the "hub" of racing in and around Charlotte, North Carolina, Mitchell moved and spent four years as the motorsports writer with the *Independent Tribune* in Concord.

Mitchell's freelance writing has been included in *Stock Car Racing* magazine, *NASCAR Magazine*, *Inside NASCAR*, *Racing Milestones*, *Last Lap*, as well as program work for Lowe's Motor Speedway and International Speedway Corporation. Some of Mitchell's technical writing has appeared on NASCAR.com.

David Poole has covered NASCAR for *The Charlotte Observer* since 1997. He has won awards for his coverage from the Associated Press Sports Editors and the National Motorsports Press Association. He was the winner of the George Cunningham Award as the NMPA's writer of the year in 2001. Poole is a graduate of the University of North Carolina and lives in his hometown of Gastonia, North Carolina, with his wife, Karen, and her three children, Matthew, David, and Emily.

Photography:
The Charlotte Observer
Brain L. Spurlock, Spurlock Photography Inc.
Joe Robbins

Editor:
Constance Holloway

Design Team:
Beth Epperly
Larry Preslar
Andrea Ross

This book is available in quantity at special discounts for your group or organization. For further information, contact:
Triumph Books
601 South LaSalle Street
Suite 500
Chicago, Illinois 60605
(312) 939-3330
Fax (312) 663-3557

Printed in the United States of America
ISBN 1-57243-557-7

CONTENTS

MARK MARTIN

Mark Martin drives the No. 6 Pfizer/Viagra Ford Taurus in the NASCAR Winston Cup Series.

Born: January 9, 1959
Hometown Born: Batesville, Arkansas
Resides: Daytona Beach, Florida
Spouse: Arlene
Children: Amy, Rachel, Heather, Stacy, and Matthew Clyde
Height: 5'6"
Weight: 135 pounds
Hobbies: Weight training, quarter-midget racing with his son

DID YOU KNOW?
Martin got his start in Winston Cup in 1981 at the track in North Wilkesboro, North Carolina. His first Winston Cup victory took place in 1989 at the Rockingham, North Carolina, race track.

CAREER HIGHLIGHTS
All-time career leader with 45 Busch Series victories. Four-time International Race of Champions series champion. Four-time champion in American Speed Association series. Has won at least one race at 17 different Winston Cup tracks. Earned $1 million bonus from Winston for his victory in the Coca-Cola 600 at Lowe's Motor Speedway at Charlotte in May of 2002.

BILL ELLIOTT

Bill Elliott drives the No. 9 Dodge in the NASCAR Winston Cup Series.

Born: October 8, 1955
Hometown: Dawsonville, Georgia
Resides: Blairsville, Georgia
Spouse: Cindy
Children: Starr, Brittany, and Chase
Height: 6'1"
Weight: 185 pounds
Hobbies: Skiing and flying

DID YOU KNOW?
Elliott has a pilot's license and is rated to fly multi-engine planes and helicopters. Elliott was named driver of the decade for the eighties in a fans poll done by ESPN. Elliott has won the National Motorsports Press Association's Most Popular Driver Award 15 times during his career.

CAREER HIGHLIGHTS
Won at Pocono and Indianapolis in 2002. Returned to victory lane in 2001 for the first time since 1994, winning the Pennzoil 400 at Homestead-Miami Speedway. Celebrated his 25th-anniversary season in 2000 driving the No. 94 Ford he also owned. Picked up his fifth career victory in 1994 at Darlington Raceway in the Southern 500 during his final season driving for Junior Johnson. Won the Winston Cup championship in 1988. Enjoyed one of the greatest seasons in Winston Cup history in 1985 by winning 11 races and 11 poles. Earned his first victory at NASCAR's top level in 1983 at Riverside International Raceway in California. Made $640 for his 1976 debut in Winston Cup racing at Rockingham.

DALE JARRETT

Dale Jarrett drives the No. 88 UPS Ford Taurus in the NASCAR Winston Cup Series.

Born: November 26, 1956
Birthplace: Newton, North Carolina
Resides: Hickory, North Carolina
Spouse: Kelley
Children: Jason, Natalee, Karsyn, and Zachary
Height: 6'2"
Weight: 215 pounds
Hobbies: Golf, other outdoor sports

DID YOU KNOW?
Jarrett became the fourth driver to win three or more Daytona 500s when he won the season opener in 2000. He earned his first Winston Cup victory in 1991 at Brooklyn, Michigan.

CAREER HIGHLIGHTS
Won 11 races and 14 poles in Busch Series competition. Seven-time competitor in the International Race of Champions series. National Motorsports Press Association driver of the year in 1997 and 1999. Won True Value Man of the Year award in 2000 for his work on behalf of the Susan G. Komen Breast Cancer Foundation and in 1996 for fundraising efforts for Brenner Children's Hospital in Winston-Salem, North Carolina, and other causes. He has won Winston Cup races at 16 different tracks in his career.

RUSTY WALLACE

In 2003 Rusty Wallace will drive the No. 2 Miller Lite Dodge in the NASCAR Winston Cup series.

Born: August 14, 1956
Birthplace: Fenton, Missouri
Resides: Lake Norman, North Carolina
Spouse: Patti
Children: Greg, Katie, and Stephen
Height: 6'
Weight: 185 pounds
Hobbies: Golf and boating

DID YOU KNOW?
Rusty Wallace is an avid aviator who owns and flies airplanes and helicopters. He says that if he weren't a Winston Cup driver, he would likely be a commercial pilot.

CAREER HIGHLIGHTS
Scored only victory of the 2001 season at California Speedway, which gave him at least one victory in 16 straight seasons. Cracked the elusive 50-win barrier at Bristol, winning the Food City 500 on March 26, 2000. Beat close friend and rival Dale Earnhardt by 12 points in 1989 to win the NASCAR Winston Cup Series championship. Won two races in 29 starts, including his first Winston Cup victory on April 6, 1986. Took 1984 Rookie-of-the-Year honors in his first full season on the NASCAR Winston Cup tour. Finished second to Earnhardt in his NASCAR Winston Cup debut on March 16, 1980.

RICKY RUDD

In 2003 Ricky Rudd will drive the No. 21 Motorcraft Ford.

Born: September 12, 1956
Birthplace: Chesapeake, Virginia
Resides: Cornelius, North Carolina
Spouse: Linda
Child: Landon Lee
Height: 5'11"
Weight: 160 pounds
Hobbies: Flying, boating, and water sports

DID YOU KNOW?
Ricky Rudd shares the modern-era record with Rusty Wallace for winning at least one race per season over 16 straight seasons. Rudd's father owned an auto salvage business that helped to spark his interest in racing. Rudd owns a classic 1932 Ford Deuce Coupe. His favorite NFL team is the Washington Redskins.

CAREER HIGHLIGHTS
In 2001 Rudd broke an 88-race winless drought with a victory in the Pocono 500 in June, his first victory since 1998. Joined the Robert Yates operation in 2000 after running his own race team for six years, and earned nearly $3 million. Withstood painful blisters and burns to win at Martinsville in September 1998. Victory in the Brickyard 400 in 1997 was his biggest as an owner and driver. Debuted his own team in 1994 after leaving Hendrick Motorsports, posting a fifth-place finish in the final standings. Posted victories in 1987 at Atlanta and Dover in his last season with Bud Moore Engineering. Scored his first career NASCAR Winston Cup Series victory in 1983. Won 1977 Winston Cup Rookie-of-the-Year honors after running in 25 races with his father's team.

TERRY LABONTE

Terry Labonte drives the No. 5 Kellogg's Chevrolet Monte Carlo in the NASCAR Winston Cup series.

Born: November 16, 1956
Birthplace: Corpus Christi, Texas
Resides: Thomasville, North Carolina
Spouse: Kim
Children: Justin and Kristen
Height: 5'7"
Weight: 165 pounds
Hobbies: Hunting

DID YOU KNOW?
In September of 2001 Terry Labonte and brother Bobby were honored in their hometown of Corpus Christi, Texas, as the only brothers to win NASCAR Winston Cup Series championships. The city renamed one of its public parks Labonte Park. Terry said it was "the proudest moment I ever had."

CAREER HIGHLIGHTS
Labonte started racing in 1964 in the quarter midgets. First Winston Cup start was the Southern 500 at the Darlington, South Carolina, Raceway in September of 1978. Won his first Winston Cup race at that track in September of 1980. Most recent Winston Cup victory was at Texas Motor Speedway in March 1999. When Labonte captured the 1984 Winston Cup Championship, he was the youngest driver (at 27 years, 11 months old) in the modern era to win that title. Total winnings through September 2002 were $29.2 million.

DARING YOUNG ROOKIE

n May of 2002, as Winston Cup teams prepared for the Coca-Cola 600 at Lowe's Motor Speedway in Charlotte, Mark Martin watched reporters chase the sport's latest story of the moment.

NASCAR's group of "young guns" drivers, who were 30 or younger at the time, had won seven of the season's first eleven races. Even though Sterling Marlin was leading the points race, it seemed that all anybody wanted to talk about was the young guys.

One young driver who'd won already was Kurt Busch, who earned his first career Cup victory at Bristol at the age of 23. Busch was Martin's teammate at Roush Racing.

"I know from up real close how good Kurt Busch is at 23," Martin said. "There are some things he can do at 23 that I can't do at 43."

Martin then tilted his head a bit.

"But," he added, "I also know there are still a few things I can do at 43 that he can't do."

If there's anybody in auto racing who knows what it's like to be a precocious young driving star, it's Mark Martin.

In 1974, when he was just 15 years old, Martin ran in more than 100 races at a track in Benton, Arkansas, near his hometown of Batesville. Many of the men he competed against were more than twice his age, yet Martin won 22 times that year.

"People forget that Jeff Gordon wasn't the first driver who was pretty good when he was young," Martin said. "I was pretty good."

He still is.

A few days after addressing the young-versus-old issue so directly at Charlotte, Martin ended a 73-race victory drought by winning the 600, Winston Cup's longest race, for the first time in his career. It was the 33rd victory in a career that began with a flourish at age 22, then flamed out two years later, forcing Martin to take a long, sometimes dreary road back into stock-car racing's major league.

At the end of the 2002 racing season Martin was 43 years old and had won more than $34 million in Winston Cup racing. He also held the all-time record for victories in the Busch Series, with 45, and had been crowned the champion of the International Race of Champions series four times.

He still, however, had not won a Winston Cup title, despite finishing in the top five in the final standings for the 10th time in his career.

"Having someone say that 'Mark Martin is the winningest driver to never win a championship,' is not a downer," he said. "What are the first words they say? 'Mark Martin is the winningest driver.' Think about it. It's however you want to take this stuff.

"I don't think I'm the best that there's ever been. If I did think that, it might be a slap in my face, but I don't. I look at what they're saying, and what they're saying is that I've done darn good."

He's been darn good ever since he was five, when his father, Julian, started giving him what can only be called a unique kind of driving lessons.

"I can remember standing on my daddy's lap, steering his car, running 80 miles an hour," Martin recalled. "We'd head toward those one-lane wooden bridges they had there in Arkansas back then and I'd scream, 'You take it! You take it!'

"He would say, 'You keep it or we're going to wreck!' He loved to see me get scared. He got a kick out of that. He was a thrill seeker."

Julian purchased bought a truck and starting hauling eggs to places such as Memphis, Tennessee, and St. Louis, Missouri. From that beginning the elder Martin gradually built his own trucking company.

"It was about 100 miles to Memphis and about 125 to Little Rock," Martin remembered. "I can remember Dad making those trips in a little over an hour over winding two-lane roads. It was always thrilling.

"Back in the early to mid-sixties the area where I grew up was like the Wild, Wild West. There was a lot of lawlessness. People did what they wanted to do, especially while driving. There wasn't a highway patrolman every 100 square miles.

"But as fast as Dad and his friends drove, they were conscious of wrecking. Whenever there was a fatal highway accident in the area, he would take me to the scene where it happened and tell me things like, 'He had two tires over the edge here and overcorrected too quickly.' But he never, never said that whoever it was that had wrecked was going too fast."

Julian Martin liked stock-car racing and often went to NASCAR events. In 1973 he took Mark with him to the Daytona 500 for the first time.

"Watching the Daytona 500 was an incredible experience," Mark said. "After we went back home he started building a car for me. It was a '55 Chevrolet six-cylinder that we planned to run in the street class on the area dirt tracks. The roll bars were made out of heavy water pipe."

The Martins painted the car "hugger" orange, a popular shade on new Camaros of the day, and put the No. 2 on the side. Mark wasn't old enough to get a license to drive, a fact that hadn't stopped him from doing it since he'd been much younger. But at 15 he was old enough to race.

He won for the first time in April of 1974 at Independence County Speedway in Locust Grove, Arkansas.

Martin still remembers how good winning felt.

"I didn't know I could win," Martin said. "It was such a thrill to go out and do something you didn't know you could do.

"We were excited and confused. We knew all along we didn't know what we were doing. There was a simplicity to life then. Anybody that wanted to talk racing, you had time to stop and tell all the stories.

"You could go to high school every day like I was doing and still do all your work on the race car. It gave you the opportunity to realize what you were doing and what you were accomplishing."

The Mark Martin Racing Team accomplished a lot that first year at tracks such as Locust Grove and the Speedbowl in Benton, Arkansas, where Martin won 22 times in 101 races—including a win in the state championship race that September.

The more the small young driver from Batesville won, the more people noticed. His name and picture kept popping up in the newspapers, and the success didn't

always sit well with his more experienced rivals.

"I faced a lot of jealousy the first few years I raced," Martin said. "We had nice-looking cars and I was 15 years old, winning races against guys who were 35 or 40."

Martin kept a diary of each race, recording where he'd finished and how much he'd won.

And he kept on winning his way up the ladder, learning to translate his dirt-track experience into success on paved tracks and taking on bigger and bigger challenges.

UPS AND DOWNS

Over the next few years Mark Martin and his race team began traveling to tracks all over the Midwest. The biggest events were part of the American Speed Association series, one of stock-car racing's traditional proving grounds.

By late in 1977 the team discovered that if it entered the final few ASA races of the season, Martin would win that year's Rookie-of-the-Year award.

The next year he won the first of three straight ASA championships, beating such drivers as Dick Trickle and another up-and-coming young star, Rusty Wallace. The toughness that would come to be a trademark of Martin's career was displayed vividly on the

way to the 1980 title when he broke his left leg, right ankle, and four bones in his left foot in a crash during an ARTGO series race in Wisconsin in early July. After Darrell Waltrip stepped in to drive one race in Martin's car as a replacement, Martin returned less than a month after his crash, set a track qualifying record, and won the race at the Milwaukee Mile using a hand clutch because of the broken left foot.

In 1981, at the age of 22, Martin was ready to tackle NASCAR. He won a pole at North Carolina Speedway in Rockingham in the Sportsman series—what's now the Busch Series—and made his first Winston Cup race in April at North Wilkesboro, North Carolina,

qualifying fifth fastest. After having mechanical trouble during that race as well as in his second start at Nashville in May, Martin went back to Indiana and reworked his race car. He returned to Nashville two months later and won that pole and another pole later that year at Richmond. In September at Talladega he won an Automobile Racing Club of America race.

Martin figured that NASCAR fame and fortune were merely a step or two away, but 1982 began a nightmarish stretch for the young man who'd known so much success so soon. A sponsor never paid its bills and Julian's trucking business suffered a downturn.

The family had borrowed every dollar it could to keep Martin racing. In April of 1983 an auctioneer sold off what was left of the Mark Martin Racing Team in the garage area at Charlotte Motor Speedway.

The next February, Martin went to Daytona with a woman named Arlene—a mother of four—whom he'd met on a blind date over the holidays and who would soon become his wife. Martin didn't have a ride for the Daytona 500, much less a garage pass.

"I stood outside and looked in and saw those drivers, and I knew I could beat them," Martin said. "And I didn't have a chance. I sunk. As low as you can sink, I sunk. And it

hurt so bad that I wound up with a chip on my shoulder about it. I was very bitter."

With no prospects on his NASCAR horizon, Martin went back to what he knew—racing on short tracks in the Midwest. Jimmy Fennig, a crew chief who'd seen Martin race in the ASA in the late seventies, suggested that the team he worked for should give Martin a call. Martin finished fourth in the 1985 ASA standings and won his fourth title in that series the following year. In 1987 he moved his family to Greensboro, North Carolina, to take a full-time ride in the NASCAR Busch series. That May he got his first Busch Series win—which was also the

first win for Ford in that series since it had been restructured in 1982—at Dover.

The years between his first foray into NASCAR and what would eventually turn out to be his successful return were hard ones for Martin. In *Mark Martin: Driven to Race*, a biography written by Bob Zeller, Martin admitted that he went from drinking very little when he was younger—and being teased about it—to drinking so much that he couldn't stop because of his problems in the early eighties.

During that 1987 Busch Series season Martin began talking to Steve Hmiel about a new Winston Cup team that might be forming for the following year. Ford officials had approached Hmiel, then working at Petty Enterprises, about starting a team for an owner who'd had success racing Fords in other series. That car owner was Jack Roush.

Roush Racing had piled up championships in sports-car racing, and Roush was ready to tackle NASCAR. When it came to picking a driver Roush talked to several candidates, but Martin stood out.

"Mark was the only one more interested in who was going to work on the car and

how much money we were going to spend on testing than about how much money he was going to make," Roush said.

Despite Martin driving and future garage area all-stars such as Hmiel and Robin Pemberton on the team, it took Roush's stock-car empire a little while to get started. Martin finished 15th in points that first season and wasn't running at the end of 10 of the season's 29 races. But Roush saw promise.

"When I was making my plans for this team, I felt that because of our Trans-Am and IMSA experience we could do a pretty good job right off," Roush said. "But then, when we actually started running in '88, I saw right away that we'd really have to hunker down to meet our expectations. Mark was pretty much carrying the team."

Late that year Martin stopped drinking alcohol. He began working out with weights, shifting his focus to a training regimen that led him to build his own gym in his Florida home, where he's often up before dawn, keeping himself in top condition for the rigors of his sport.

During the next season Martin was a consistent front-runner in Winston Cup, finishing in the top five with a regularity that made him a challenger for the championship despite never having won a race in the series. He finished second five times and third four times, but had seen things like blistered tires, loose lug nuts, and fuel-mileage miscalculations cost him potential victories.

That changed in October at Rockingham. He pulled away from Rusty Wallace after a restart with 20 laps left in a crash-filled race and earned his first Cup victory in his 113th start.

"I can't believe it!" Martin said as tears welled in his eyes in victory lane. "My life is fulfilled. At the end of the race I was wondering what would go wrong. I even figured I might run my car into the wall and lose it. It has felt like we were in a duel with fate and always lost. Fate was on our side this time."

DRIVEN TO WIN

After Mark Martin scored one of what would be his three 1989 victories (in a race at Richmond), NASCAR slapped his team with the largest fine in the sport's history to that point—$40,000—for a carburetor spacer plate that was higher than allowed. More important, it docked the team 46 points, the difference between Martin's first-place finish and what he would have earned for being the last car on the lead lap.

"It's like running a stop sign when nothing is coming, but a policeman catches you and writes you up," Martin said the next day, contending that the part gave his team no competitive edge in the race. "You broke the law and you have to pay for it, but this is like getting the death penalty for it."

He didn't know how right he would be. Martin led the points race by 45 points with two races to go, but Earnhardt won at Phoenix and regained the lead. Martin finished second in the final standings to Earnhardt, just 26 points behind—fewer points than the 46 his team had been docked by NASCAR.

Had the penalty cost Martin and Roush the title? It certainly hadn't helped, of course, but the team created some of its own problems—most notably testing several of its Fords at Atlanta Motor Speedway, the site of the season finale, before borrowing a car from Robert Yates Racing for that last race. It was

a decision that many experts would second-guess for years to come.

"There's no doubt in my mind that I made decisions that hurt my chances, based on how bad I wanted [to win,]" Martin would say years later.

Martin would finish second in points again in 1994 and once more in 1998 in what ranks as his best career season. He won seven times that year, twice more than the five victories he had in 1993—his previous best effort—but never had much of a chance to win the title because Jeff Gordon won 13 times.

Martin took pride in the 1998 season because of the upheaval he and his team had been through in the previous two years. After Martin's first year without a Cup victory since 1989, Steve Hmiel moved to another position within Roush Racing after the 1996 season along with Jimmy Fennig, the crew chief who'd helped Martin get the break in his return to the ASA series in 1986.

Martin won four races and finished third in the standings in 1997, behind Gordon and Dale Jarrett in the closest three-way points finish in the sport's modern era. During the next off season Fennig and another member of the team picked up and moved along with Martin from a Roush Racing shop in Liberty, North Carolina, to one in Mooresville, North Carolina.

When Martin won at Las Vegas in the third race of that season, he said it was one of the highlights of his career.

"People want to work for winning teams," Martin said. "Winning is the glue that holds it together. It holds the sponsors, it holds all the great people who work on my car. It's the glue

that sticks them. Without the winning, the glue can hold only so long.

"That's one of the miseries that go with the sport for me. Nothing is ever enough. A very short spell of lackluster performance and my confidence goes all to heck. As far as I am concerned, confidence is not worth a whole lot if you're not giving the performance. You have to give the performance. You have to do all you can do all of the time.

"I don't love to race; I love to win. I don't race to drive. I don't like driving cars. I don't like driving cars fast. I like winning. That's why I do it. I wouldn't ever go to the race track just to take a car around the track. Never. That's not why I drive race cars. I drive race cars to win, not because it's fun to drive the car."

Martin would go without a victory again in 2001, and after that season he once again went through a major change. Fennig and Martin's crew from that season swapped places with

Ben Leslie and his crew, with Leslie's group moving from Busch's team in Roush Racing. The win at Charlotte in May of 2002 was that group's first taste of victory, and Martin was happy to bring it to them.

"That was a unique win," he said. "I will never get to win my first Winston Cup race again, but that's the closest thing to the first win I had. And the next closest was the win we had at Las Vegas in 1998 three races out of the box with a new team.

"Those wins were great in my book because I'm able to share that experience, that enthusiasm, and that excitement with them. I get to feel like they did it; it was their package, but I got to deliver it to them. They're the ones who did it, but someone still has to drop it off on your doorstep. Having the honor to deliver it was really special to me."

STRONG SURVIVOR

Winning, in all of its forms, is special to Martin. He is proud to have the most career victories in the Busch Series. He also especially cherishes his four IROC titles.

"That's huge to me," he said. "There ain't no fuel mileage, there ain't no pit stops, there ain't no bunch of junk. It's just line them up and go, boys.

"To tell you that is like bragging, and I am not bragging. I am just saying . . . it's just the driver. All that other stuff is taken out of it. It has been pretty sweet. It's not a Winston Cup championship. But you know something? The most important thing in racing, I think, is respect. Somebody who could look at that and

not respect that, I don't know what you have to do to get it."

Though Martin does not have a Winston Cup championship trophy in his case, he does have other people's respect. Whenever his fellow drivers are asked to name a driver they'd like to have as a teammate or one whose talents they admire, Martin consistently finishes at the top of those lists.

"I've tried to do what I thought was the right thing along the way," Martin said. "I've had a lot of success but not as much as some. One of the byproducts of me racing my guts out and giving my all week in and week out, but still trying to treat people the way I wanted to be treated on the race track and

have my share of success at the same time, is respect from the competitors."

Once again in 2002 Martin had the points lead late in the year. Once again he started to face the questions about never having been first at the end of a season. And once again he answered the questions the same way.

"We can only work on the stuff we can control," he said. "All we can do is try to score the most points. It won't ruin my life if we never get first. It won't make my life if we do. I won't be a better driver the morning after the season's final race if I have that trophy sitting next to me.

"Would I be proud to win it? You'd better believe it. Everybody wants to be the best. That's one grand measure of it. But I have done some of the dumbest things, I have made some of the biggest mistakes you can make. And I have had the greatest days anybody has ever experienced. The sun always came up the next day.

"Don't get me wrong; it means a lot to me. But you have to live . . . you have to go on, no matter what. You need to take the good with appreciation and you need to accept the misfortunes the same way."

Martin certainly has known his share of both.

In August of 1998, during the greatest single season of his son's racing career, Julian Martin died in the crash of a private plane he was piloting in eastern Nevada. Julian's wife (Mark's stepmother), Shelley, and their 11-year-old daughter, Sarah, were also killed.

Mark Martin, who raced and finished fourth the next week at Michigan and won the race the following weekend at Bristol, dedicated that victory to the memory of his father and his family.

There must have been an awful sense of déjà vu for Martin in April of 2002 when he heard that Roush, piloting an experimental plane, had crashed into a lake near Troy, Alabama. Roush had been trapped upside down in the cockpit underwater and would have drowned if not for Larry Hicks, an ex-

Marine. Hicks, who lived on the shoreline of the lake, rescued and revived Roush who, despite serious injuries to his leg, survived and has made a full recovery.

"I wouldn't let myself think about what it was going to be like if Jack wasn't going be there," Martin said of that long first night following Roush's crash when a full recovery barely seemed possible. "It didn't look good.

"Jack's got my back, like a father would have. It's good to have that. I don't have a dad anymore. I won't replace the relationship I have with Jack; I don't see that happening in my life, ever having a relationship that can get that deep again. I didn't need to lose that. It's personal."

Racing is still a big part of Martin's life and, if he has anything to say about it, it will be that way for a long time. He helped recruit Matt Kenseth to the Roush Racing stable and

28

LEGENDS OF NASCAR

has partial ownership with Roush of the team for which Kurt Busch drives. He's also involved in the development of Busch's younger brother, Kyle, who raced in the ASA series in 2002 and plans to move into NASCAR's truck series in 2003.

Another young driver has caught Martin's eye as well. In 1991 Arlene gave birth to a son. Matt Martin is already showing promise that he'll follow in his father's footsteps in quarter-midget and Legends car racing.

In perhaps another 15 years, will Matt Martin be turning up the pressure on veteran Winston Cup stars such as Busch, Ryan Newman, Jimmie Johnson, and Dale Earnhardt Jr.? Only time will tell.

For now, Martin is content with where he's been and confident about where he's going.

"I'm happy with who I am," Martin said. "I don't know who I would be or what I would be like if I hadn't gone through all of the things I went through. Without all the nightmares and the horrors, I would not be the same person.

"The roads I went down took me to Arlene, to Jack Roush, and have made me appreciate the opportunities that I have had. I am happy with where I am today and who I am today, and I am thankful for having survived all that I survived."

BILL ELLIOTT

HUMBLE ROOTS

Part of the history of NASCAR is the fact that the sport grew from dirt track racing on Friday and Saturday nights into a multibillion-dollar industry that travels across the country and entertains over 100,000 passionate race fans on an almost weekly basis.

If ever there was a driver who has just about seen it all—both good times and bad—it's 27-year Winston Cup veteran Bill Elliott. Having grown up in rural Dawsonville, Georgia, the redheaded Elliott still maintains that Southern, low-key demeanor that has made him one of the most popular drivers in Winston Cup

history. Elliott has been voted the most popular driver in Winston Cup racing on a record 15 different occasions.

At age 47, in a sport where a premium has been put on young drivers with potential, Elliott is still getting the job done behind the wheel of the No. 9 Dodge owned by Ray Evernham.

Elliott started from scratch, driving for a family-owned operation. Through it all he has seemingly changed very little. He still appreciates the same things that young racers do: a good car and a chance to win on any given Sunday. Yet he admits that Winston Cup competition has changed a great deal.

"Looking back over it, it just seems like it was yesterday when I got started," Elliott said. "Day in and day out, I still enjoy the racing. It's a lot of fun. It's gotten awful competitive the last couple of years. It's awful tough from that side. These younger drivers make you work a little harder, but that's what it's all about."

Elliott, thanks to his age, is now racing the proverbial clock and knows the time will come for him to retire from the Winston Cup Series.

"It's been a lot of fun," Elliott acknowledged. "As many years as I've been doing it, I'm very fortunate to still be here. You look back, and we've seen a lot of situations the last 20-some-odd years in this sport, especially with the deal that happened to Dale Earnhardt. I've been very fortunate, very lucky, and proud to accomplish what I've done the last number of years. To race all the guys that I've raced against through the years has been unique."

Elliott is rather unique. After winning 40 races and 49 poles throughout his storied career, Elliott went through a six-year winless drought that had many inside the garage area wondering if "Awesome Bill" had reached his peak. In 2001, for example, his victory at Homestead-Miami Speedway allowed him to become only the 70th driver in Winston Cup history to win a race at over 45 years of age.

It's hard for veterans in any sport to just roll over and watch youth come in and prevail right away, but it's something that Elliott has come to terms with.

"Week in and week out, the veterans understand point racing a little better than the younger guys," Elliott said. "I think that's a key. A little bit of patience in the race can go a long way as far as where a car won't stick or where it doesn't need to be. I think that's one side of the coin. On the other hand, it's hard to tell young guys that haven't been around these tracks much what to expect. Sometimes that's a factor, but there are a lot of older guys that have good equipment, too, and they're in good cars.

"A lot of young guys like Kevin Harvick have come in and teach us a little bit of something. It's never black and white."

Once a freckle-faced youngster living in the north Georgia hills, Elliott overcame his meager beginnings through hard work and determination. His father, George, owned a building-supply company, a Ford dealership, and parcels of land. The three Elliott boys were raised in a "strict manner."

"You didn't smoke, drink, or party," explained Bill's brother, Ernie Elliott. "You also came straight home from school each day and went to work."

At the age of nine, Bill Elliott was put to work operating a forklift; three years later he was driving a truck. By his senior year in high school, Elliott transferred to a school that allowed students who had jobs to be dismissed at noon. Once he left school, Elliott headed to work at his father's dealership where his other brother, Dan, ran the parts department.

Bill and Ernie Elliott kept busy working and servicing cars in the back of the shop.

All three of George Elliott's sons shared a love of racing, but it was Bill who seemed to have the gift and was a natural behind the wheel of a stock car.

"Bill never really had to work at driving a race car," Ernie Elliott said.

Bill Elliott started driving Georgia short tracks before he graduated from high school but failed to qualify for the first two sports-man races he entered at Charlotte Motor

Speedway in 1974–1975. Later, after watching Bill's success on various Georgia short tracks, it became clear to his father that Bill was ready to move to the next plateau.

On February 29, 1976, Elliott Racing rolled into Rockingham, North Carolina, as a family-owned operation, with Bill Elliott making his first career Winston Cup start. It was a small effort—compared to many of the other teams and drivers—with one car, two motors, volunteers making up the pit crew, and tons of determination. For his first start at

NASCAR's top level, Elliott earned a meager—by today's standards—$640.

It was a starting point for Elliott Racing, which ran seven more races throughout 1976, with the underfunded team failing to finish in five of eight starts. Over the next three seasons, Elliott ran ten races per year for his father's team and picked up an extra four races in 1979 with former team owner Roger Hamby. Throughout that time, Elliott was showing great promise, with a best finish of second.

Elliott continued to drive for his family for the 1980–1981 seasons, but he got one of his biggest breaks in 1982 when wealthy team owner Harry Melling purchased his dad's team and asked him to remain as the driver. Elliott won his first Winston Cup pole and finished second on three occasions.

The rest, as they say, is history.

In 1983, his first full season on the Winston Cup tour, Elliott and Melling won their first race together at the Riverside, California, 117th start. At year's end, the pairing had amassed 11 top-five finishes and ended up third in the final Winston Cup point standings.

The 1984 season was also a solid one, as Elliott won four races, three poles, and again finished third in the points race. Nobody could have imagined what the No. 9 Melling Ford would pull off the following year.

RACING TO HISTORY

For years Bill Elliott had been known as "Awesome Bill from Dawsonville." In 1985 his moniker seemed all the more fitting.

That year the wins came early and often, totaling 11 victories by the end of the season. The 11 trips to victory lane, however, weren't the only major story for Elliott that year. By winning three of the four major races that season, Elliott won a $1 million bonus through R. J. Reynolds' Winston Million program.

While the significance of his win in NASCAR's biggest race was huge, the 1985 Daytona 500 victory only set the stage for a season that will go down in history for Elliott.

Later that year at Talladega, Elliott scored another major victory.

In only his third season on the Winston Cup tour, Elliott was quickly becoming a household name among many people who had never paid much attention to stock-car racing. The pressure was very evident on the face of Elliott, who would later admit that it got the best of him. Three years earlier, the people who had wanted to interview Elliott could have been counted on one hand. All of a sudden, the racing media were tracking his every move.

When the Winston Cup tour rolled into Charlotte for the Coca-Cola 600, Elliott's tire went flat and a loose lug nut ripped a hole in a brake line. He ended up with an 18th-place

finish, 21 laps behind race winner Darrell Waltrip. As a result Elliott's only chance at the bonus came down to his performance at Darlington Raceway for the 1985 Southern 500.

Media outlets that had never expressed an interest in NASCAR were asking for credentials. The scene when Elliott showed up at the tricky South Carolina track was a wild one. Keep in mind that a shy Southern guy who was only in his junior season of Winston Cup racing was facing intense scrutiny from the time practice and qualifying began on Friday until he was strapped into his car that warm Sunday afternoon.

The frenzy bothered Elliott in a big way. Having to give so many interviews created a distraction from his goal of winning the race and picking up the bonus.

"I was pretty resentful of the media," Elliott recalled. "A lot of the people didn't write exactly what I said, and I blamed it a lot on the media, which a lot of it wasn't their fault. I couldn't communicate well. I didn't know how to communicate. It became a situation that I let get to me."

It got so bad at Darlington that the highway patrol shielded him from the onslaught. According to some drivers, Elliott took the situation a little too far.

"In my opinion they totally overreacted," says retired Winston Cup champion Darrell Waltrip. "They started having guards in roped-off areas. It was, 'You can talk to Bill at this time, and don't talk to him at any other time.' Looking back, they didn't handle it very well."

As a result of his numerous victories, Elliott made it to Darlington with the Winston Cup championship lead over Waltrip. While Elliott was making himself scarce, Waltrip took full advantage of the situation and began to play mind games.

"We were pretty hard on him," Waltrip said. "We wanted to win the championship because that was the only thing that was left for us. We

turned the heat up every which way we could to make sure they knew they were in another battle."

The verbal barbs worked perfectly, sending Elliott to seek the advice of racing legend Richard Petty.

"I don't remember what I told him, but it didn't help," Petty says. "Bill was like a kid coming out of college, signing a $2 million to $3 million bonus to play sports. All of a sudden he had all this media attention. He didn't know how to handle or cope with it."

As if scripted by Hollywood, Elliott's day played out before a sold-out crowd that had filed into the grandstands at the 1.366-mile track. For much of the race Elliott just stayed in sight of the leaders and didn't press the issue. Now-retired legend Cale Yarborough was leading until late in the race, when he experienced mechanical failures that allowed Elliott to take a lead he would never relinquish.

Through all the adversity of trying to win the Winston Million, Elliott had pulled off the feat. Fireworks were set off afterward, balloons were released, and fake million-dollar bills were thrown around in victory lane.

For one of the first times in his career, Elliott was left nearly speechless after winning the biggest purse in NASCAR history.

"Man, what a day," Elliott said.

Ernie Elliott, who was an active member of the Melling team, said he wouldn't go through what they went through at Darlington again, no matter how much money was on the line.

"If I had to do it over again, I don't think I would," he said. "It took us out of something where we weren't in the spotlight to where we were in a lot of spotlight. We were scrutinized by everyone and it made it very difficult to concentrate."

In 1985 Elliott was clearly the man to beat. His inconsistency, however, allowed Waltrip to hang around in the championship battle for the remaining races of the season. When all was said and done, Waltrip prevailed to win his third and final NASCAR Winston Cup championship.

"It seemed like from Darlington on, they really let their guard down," Waltrip said. "They put everything they had [into] winning the million, but didn't have enough staying power to win the championship."

BEST OF THE BEST

Now firmly established as a legitimate threat to win every weekend, Bill Elliott focused on winning the Winston Cup championship. After coming up short in 1985, expectations were high heading into the 1986 campaign.

The goals of Elliott and the Melling team would not be met as they struggled with only a pair of wins at Michigan to finish ninth in the final standings. Elliott also won The Winston All-Star race at Charlotte.

Elliott returned to his winning and consistent form in 1987, winning six races and finishing second in the standings once again.

The best year of Elliott's career came in 1988, when he and the Melling team won three races and headed into the final race of the season at Atlanta, trying to protect a 79-point championship lead over Rusty Wallace. Entering the race, Elliott needed to finish only 18th and the title would be his, regardless of what Wallace did.

With that in mind, the Melling team prepared Elliott's car to make it the full 500-mile distance rather than to contend for the victory. It was a move that almost cost the team the $1 million championship purse as Wallace won the race and Elliott struggled to finish 11th, only 24 points ahead of Wallace but good enough to earn him the 1988 Winston Cup title.

"I did everything in my power," Wallace said afterward. "To come so close yet be so far

away, I'm pretty dejected. Bill's a good friend of mine and I congratulated him like I promised I would. But the way he drove got to me; it was maddening."

The conservative strategy was widely criticized by the media, too, but Elliott defended his cautious approach.

"I did what I had to do," Elliott said. "I did what any other driver in the same position would have done. It's a relief it's over. Rusty will be in my position some day and have to do the same thing. It'll all come back to him."

Ironically, Elliott's comments would ring true the following season as Wallace entered the season finale at Atlanta, trying to protect a slim points lead. While he struggled in the race, Wallace would end up winning the 1989 Winston Cup championship by a scant 12 points over Dale Earnhardt. Elliott finished

that season with three wins to finish sixth in the final standings.

The 1990 season was somewhat of a disappointment for Elliott. The Melling camp earned only one victory to finish fourth in the championship battle. Unhappy with his team's performance, Elliott made one of the toughest decisions of his life, announcing that the 1991 season would be his last with the Melling organization, and that he would drive for legendary team owner Junior Johnson in 1992. Elliott finished 11th in the standings.

The teaming of Elliott with Johnson's team, based out of Wilkes County, North Carolina, was one that many expected big things from. As it turned out, Elliott won five times to head into the final race of the season with a chance to win his second Winston Cup title.

44

From the start, many knew the pairing was one that struck fear among their rivals.

"For the rest of the drivers, I think it was a bad day," retired racing legend Buddy Baker said of the union. "If either one of them ever wrote a book, it wouldn't be but two pages in it. They do most of their talking on the race track."

The 1992 championship came down to the final race of the season with a handful of drivers, including Elliott, in contention for the title. Davey Allison came into the race with the lead but got caught up in a wreck that dropped him out of the fight. That opened the door for the race between Kulwicki and Elliott. Kulwicki led Elliott by a single lap. The difference in that one circuit around the Atlanta track allowed Kulwicki to win the championship by a mere 10 points. It remains the closest final points margin in Winston Cup history.

"I was aware of what was at stake, but I'd have raced just as hard for a dollar," Elliott said. "I was just relieved it was over."

After coming so close to the title the year prior, the 1993 campaign left a lot to be desired. Elliott failed to win a race that year, which snapped a 10-year streak of at least one victory per season. He ended the season eighth in the final point standings. With things not getting a lot better in 1994, Elliott announced that his third season with Johnson would be his final year and that he was forming his own race team for the 1995 season. Elliott scored a victory in the spring race at Darlington, but that was about all the team had to celebrate as he concluded his stint with Johnson 10th in points.

When Elliott arrived at Daytona in 1995 he was not only the driver but also the team owner. Being both the owner and driver was a popular trend, but Elliot had not anticipated

the extra duties that performing both jobs required.

The growing pains for Elliott's new team were obvious from the start as he went through a second-straight season without a win and a best finish of fourth on two occasions. He ended up with an eighth-place finish in the final standings. Just when Elliott thought things could only get better in the 1996 season, he broke his left thighbone in a multicar crash at Talladega. As a result Elliott missed seven races during his recovery and finished 30th in the championship battle.

Elliott bounced back nicely in 1997 to finish eighth in the final standings but later failed to finish in the top 15 the following three years. Seeing the proverbial writing on the wall, Elliott decided to close the doors on his race team at the end of the 2000 season.

"There are days this sport will eat you alive," Elliott said.

CAREER REJUVENATION

Bill Elliott got the opportunity of a lifetime in 2001 when he joined Evernham Motorsports to help spearhead manufacturer Dodge's return to the NASCAR Winston Cup Series. After great success as Jeff Gordon's crew chief at Hendrick Motorsports, Ray Evernham was looking for another challenge—which he got in a big way by building a team from scratch.

Instead of having to worry about the business side of running his own race team, Elliott wanted to focus solely on driving like he did in his glory days with the Melling operation. Before he ever announced drivers for his two-car Dodge team, Evernham made it clear that he was looking for one veteran and one young driver.

After the formalities and contracts were ironed out, Elliott joined forces with Evernham and rookie driver Casey Atwood.

As it turned out, in his 26th year on the Winston Cup tour Elliott still had the heart and desire that race fans hadn't seen since his 1994 victory at Darlington.

In his first race with the Evernham team Elliott shocked more than a few of his critics by winning the pole for the season-opening Daytona 500 before finishing fifth in NASCAR's most prestigious race.

With only three races remaining in the 2001 season, it looked as if Elliott's losing skid would continue through a seventh straight year. But when the Winston Cup tour rolled into

Homestead-Miami Speedway, Elliott had the fastest car in qualifying and earned his second pole of the season for the Pennzoil 400. Atwood qualified second to make it an all-Evernham front row start at the south Florida track.

Atwood was leading in the late stages and looking for his very first Winston Cup victory while Elliott was running a close second. With fewer than five laps to go, Atwood's car bobbled and Elliott slipped by to take the victory and end a 227-race losing skid in a hugely popular win among race fans.

"It was just a great day for all of the guys on this team," Elliott said following his return to

victory lane. "It's not just *I*, it's *we*. We've worked hard and been through a lot of rough times this year. So to come here and sit on the pole and win the race is fantastic. This is great. The relationship I've had with Ray Evernham this year has been fantastic because he stood behind me through thick and thin, and that's the kind of team owner I want."

Elliott said he was unsure whether he would win another Winston Cup race after years of frustration and bad luck.

"I was beginning to think Ray Evernham didn't make a very good decision," Elliott said.

"You get to the point where you don't think you'll ever win another race."

Elliott would finish the 2001 season 15th in the final Winston Cup points standings.

If the 2002 Winston Cup season had a major story line, it was the invasion and success of the young drivers. As the youth movement gained attention, the 47-year-old Elliott was piecing together one of his best seasons in years and was showing everybody he was still a factor every week.

It used to take years for a new driver to gain the knowledge needed to win at the Winston Cup level. But with the tremendous success of the "young guns" drivers, such as Dale Earnhardt Jr., Tony Stewart, Matt Kenseth, Jimmie Johnson, and Ryan Newman, it has become evident that putting young talent into winning equipment was enough to get the job done.

"It's gotten very competitive and tough to win the last few years," Elliott said. "These younger drivers have made us old guys work a little harder. It's just harder to stay consistent nowadays with the new guys that don't know what it used to take to win races. A lot of the veterans have a habit of doing things a certain way and it can be hard to break. It's like trying to teach an old dog new tricks."

By August of 2002 Elliott was back to his form of old and had three poles when the Winston Cup tour rolled into Pocono for the fall race at the 2.5-mile triangular track. Just as he had the previous year at Miami, Elliott started from the pole and, in dominating fashion, pulled off his first victory of the season.

Only a week later Elliott would pick up one of the greatest victories of his career by winning the Brickyard 400 at the legendary Indianapolis Motor Speedway after slipping ast fellow veteran Rusty Wallace. It was the 3rd victory of what has been a legendary effort n the part of Elliott.

"This is as good as it gets," Elliott said fterward. "To win at Indianapolis is incredile. All these guys on this team make it appen every week and that's what it's all bout. I'm so proud of my guys. It's so emoonal because it seems like it's taken a lifetime get here. I don't know how to describe it. ven the years when I owned my own team, I an well; but I never could make the right deciions to get into victory lane. Every time it was lways a hard-luck story why I didn't win. Now know in my own mind that I can do it each nd every week."

A PREORDAINED PATH

Crossroads.

You don't find them on race tracks.

In one form or another, a track is really a great big circle and there's only one direction.

There are no ambiguities, no choices. There is no this way or that way.

There's only forward.

Life, of course, isn't that easy. Every door you open brings you to a thousand other doors. Every path you choose takes you to another fork in the road. You do the best you can and hope you get the really big decisions right more often than you get them wrong.

Dale Jarrett knows all of this, firsthand.

The 1999 Winston Cup champion is one of the most accomplished and respected drivers in NASCAR history. He'll make his 500th career start in stock-car racing's top division early in the 2003 season. He has thirty victories, with three of those wins coming in the Daytona 500, the sport's premier event.

He has stood center stage at the annual Winston Cup awards ceremony in New York City with applause washing over him and his family and confetti raining down on their heads. He brought one of the sport's most highly regarded car owners,

JARRETT

Robert Yates, a championship he richly deserved after years of toil and heartbreak.

It could be argued, of course, that Jarrett's path to stock-car stardom was clear from the day he was born, November 26, 1956, in the small North Carolina town of Newton.

His father, Ned, was already driving in NASCAR races when Dale was born. By the time Dale turned three, Ned had won his first two races in what was then known as the Grand National division. Before Dale was old enough for first grade, Ned was the sport's champion.

Ned would win 50 races in his career and add a second championship in 1965 before retiring from the driver's seat and moving on to a long, successful career in broadcasting that, many years later, allowed him to share directly in one of his son's greatest moments.

Ned Jarrett also became a track promoter, running the historic Hickory Motor Speedway. Dale worked at the track on

weekends and was responsible for keeping the grass cut through the week.

Thinking it would save him some time with the latter chore, Jarrett once convinced his father to buy a goat. The goat, however, ate everything he could get to—except for grass, that is.

Jarrett played football, basketball, and golf at Newton-Conover High School, excelling at all three sports. It wasn't until after he graduated that he finally developed an interest in racing. He ran his first race in 1977 at Hickory in a car he worked on with friends Andy Petree, now a Winston Cup team owner, and Jimmy Newsome.

Jarrett started last and finished ninth in the 25-lap race, earning $35.

And he was hooked.

"It was just unbelievable," Jarrett said. "I had no idea. I literally ran from down on the track upstairs and told my mom and dad, 'I found it! This is what I want to do!'"

And so, Jarrett had chosen his path.

THE ULTIMATE MOMENT

Dale Jarrett went into racing with no illusions. He knew how tough the sport could be, how much hard work it demanded. He also knew that opportunities would not come easily. Although his father had been the sport's champion twice, racing in that era had not been a particularly lucrative line of work. Whereas today's Winston Cup champion gets a check for more than $3 million at the end of the season, Ned Jarrett collected a prize of $6,000 for one of his titles. Dale Jarrett wouldn't be racing on Daddy's money.

"We raced on just what little money we could get," Jarrett said. "People assumed a lot of times that because I was Ned Jarrett's son that we had plenty of money and didn't have to worry about it. That certainly was not the case."

Jarrett didn't win at Hickory until 1980, when he was 23—an age at which some of today's young stars have already won hundreds of times on their way up the developmental ladder.

He moved to the Busch Grand National series in 1982, the first year NASCAR's second-tier series carried that name. In his first four seasons there, Jarrett raced 120 times and finished in the top 10 in 72 of those starts. Finally, in 1986, in his 142nd start, he

won at Orange County Speedway in Rougemont, North Carolina, a .375-mile short track.

Racing in the Busch series provided Jarrett with the kind of experience that only seat time can provide. He got his first win on a super-speedway at Charlotte in May of 1988. In all he won 11 races in more than 300 career Busch series starts.

Jarrett made his first career Winston Cup start at Martinsville in 1984 but didn't get his first shot at that series on a regular basis until 1987, when he started 24 races in cars owned by Mike Freedlander.

As that season came to a close Jarrett and his wife, Kelley, were expecting their first child together—Jarrett's oldest son, Jason, is from his first marriage. By the time Natalee

was born the next March her father was driving cars owned by three-time Winston Cup champion Cale Yarborough. Jarrett was hired to drive the 19 races Yarborough didn't plan to drive in what would be his final season behind the wheel, and when Yarborough retired in 1989 Jarrett took over full time.

Kelley was expecting her second child late that year, too. As the 1989 season came to a close, Yarborough announced that he had hired Dick Trickle for 1990. Jarrett had no Winston Cup ride.

Early the next season, however, Neil Bonnett was involved in a wreck during a race at Darlington while driving a Ford owned by the Wood Brothers. Bonnett suffered from amnesia after the crash and the Woods needed a driver for the April 8 race at Bristol. Jarrett was hired for one race—three days before Kelley gave birth to another daughter, named Karsyn—and wound up staying for two years.

"It was more than me being a race driver for them," Jarrett said of the Wood Brothers, who've fielded cars for many of the greatest drivers in NASCAR history. "They made me feel like I was a part of their family." Jarrett had seven top-10 finishes for the Wood Brothers in 1990, including a career-best fourth at Atlanta. He was running well enough again in 1991 to attract attention from Washington Redskins coach Joe Gibbs, who had decided to start his own Winston Cup team in 1992. On the Tuesday before the

season's second race at Michigan, Jarrett was named the driver for Gibbs' cars.

Then he went to Michigan and edged Davey Allison by less than a foot to win the Champion 400 at Michigan for his first career Winston Cup victory in 129 starts.

Jarrett had raced side-by-side with Allison for the final two laps, winning at the line against the son of Bobby Allison in a battle of second-generation NASCAR drivers. It was the 95th victory for the Wood Brothers, but their first since 1987—a stretch of 154 races.

"If you're a driver, you sit around and imagine what these things would be like," Jarrett said. "It felt even better than I thought it would."

There was a huge celebration after that victory in the Wood Brothers' hometown of Stuart, Virginia, but for Jarrett there was a bittersweet tinge. He was leaving to join the Gibbs team, with brother-in-law Jimmy Makar as his crew chief. It was a brand-new team. Once more, at age 35, Jarrett was making a new start.

The first year was far from a disaster— eight top-10 finishes including a second-place finish at Bristol—but the task of finding success with a start-up team was daunting. Jarrett also had surgery on a disc in his back after the 1992 season, so when he went to Daytona to start his second year with Joe Gibbs Racing, question marks hung in the air.

It's difficult to adequately explain how important Daytona International Speedway is in the culture of NASCAR. When the

2.5-mile track was built in 1959 in the city where NASCAR was founded, it was bigger and faster than anything anybody in stock-car racing had ever seen. The 500-mile race run there every February instantly became the sport's biggest stage.

When Dale Jarrett was seven years old, he was in the infield watching when his father ran out of gas while leading late in the Daytona 500. That would be as close as Ned would ever come to winning his sport's biggest race.

In February 1993, with Ned in the television booth calling the race as an analyst for CBS Sports, Dale Jarrett found himself running behind the sport's biggest name, Dale Earnhardt, and a rookie who would soon become NASCAR's top star, Jeff Gordon, with only three laps left in the 500. Jarrett pulled around Gordon and drew even with

Earnhardt on the next-to-last lap of the 188-lap race. Geoffrey Bodine lined up behind Jarrett, giving Jarrett's car the drafting push it needed to pass Earnhardt for the lead.

Up in the booth Ned Jarrett's fellow announcers fell quiet. They wanted to let a father call his son's ultimate moment.

"You've got it!" Ned said. "Dale Jarrett is going to win the Daytona 500."

Dale Jarrett did exactly that.

"I realized that the Daytona 500 was the biggest show in NASCAR Winston Cup racing," he would say a week later in describing the publicity whirlwind that followed his victory. "But I doubt any driver really realizes how big it is. I've never experienced the kind of demands on my time that winning the Daytona 500 has brought. But it's the good kind . . . the kind of demands you don't mind."

HIGHS AND LOWS

Although Dale Jarrett's win at the Daytona 500 would be the team's only victory in 1993, Jarrett finished fourth in the final driver's standings and seemed to be poised to help his team take a place among the sport's top-level operations. But once more, the path to the top would not be that straight of a line. He'd had 13 top-five and 18 top-10 finishes in 1993, but 1994 turned into a terrible struggle. The low point came when he failed to qualify for a race at North Wilkesboro, North Carolina, in October.

"I sat on the couch and watched the North Wilkesboro race on TV and felt like I was at the bottom of the ocean," Jarrett said. "Our team was too good to be missing races."

The turnaround couldn't have come more swiftly. One week after missing that race, Jarrett won at Charlotte, snapping a 54-race winless streak. Still, the team finished only 16th in the standings that year with just nine top-10 finishes, half as many as it had posted the year before.

Jarrett decided to leave Joe Gibbs Racing to start his own team, a challenge several other drivers were taking on after driver/owner Alan Kulwicki's surprise run to the 1992 championship showed the possibilities. Kelley was pregnant again, after all—Zachary would be born in December—so it had to be time for another major change in direction for her husband's career.

During the 1994 season, however, Ernie Irvan was seriously injured in a crash during a practice session at Michigan. Irvan had been hired to drive the No. 28 Ford owned by Robert Yates late in 1993 after Davey Allison, the driver whom Jarrett had edged at Michigan for his first win back in 1991, had been killed in a helicopter crash. Now, Yates needed a driver for his cars because Irvan, who'd beaten the odds by surviving his crash, faced a long, uncertain recovery before returning to NASCAR competition.

"Robert's team is among the top two or three in the sport," Jarrett said at the time. "I feel I've paid my dues for a chance with that type of team, a title contender. It's not that Joe Gibbs Racing won't get there. It's that Robert Yates Racing is there now."

Jarrett said he owed Gibbs a huge debt, not only for giving him a ride in good cars but for

providing a role model to help him learn some important lessons.

But Jarrett felt he was being led to the Yates team, so he agreed to drive the No. 28 in 1995. If Irvan could make it back, Yates would field a second car for Jarrett for the rest of that year; then Jarrett could revive his plans to start his own team for 1996.

"I decided I needed to make the move one night while watching *SportsCenter* on ESPN," Jarrett said. "They were talking about some baseball player and said his situation was day-to-day. I thought to myself, 'Really, aren't we all in a day-to-day situation?' At that minute that was the best opportunity for '95. I could worry about '96 later on."

It seemed like a great decision when Jarrett won the pole for the Daytona 500, but things went quickly downhill from there.

The No. 28 team had been Allison's team; then it had been Irvan's. And it would, if Irvan completed his miraculous comeback, be Irvan's team again. No matter how much horsepower a Robert Yates–built engine could make, it couldn't generate chemistry. By May at Charlotte, things had come to a boiling point.

After a meeting to discuss the team's problems, Jarrett was offered a chance to resign. He elected to tough it out, hoping things would get better and knowing that it would be much harder to find a sponsor for the team he wanted to start in 1996 if he got kicked out of his ride.

Just a few weeks later Jarrett nursed his last tank of fuel over the final laps of a race at Pocono Raceway and held on to score his first victory for Robert Yates Racing. His car sputtered as it came off the final turn and ran out of gas as he took the checkered flag. He had to

get pushed by other cars to get back to victory lane.

"I've got to admit this win takes a lot of pressure off," Jarrett said. "I didn't want to be the only guy who drove Robert's car for a full season without winning."

Shortly after that victory, however, Yates indicated to Jarrett that his plans for 1996 didn't include two teams. Irvan was almost ready to come back, so that meant Jarrett faced another difficult choice.

"Robert said, 'They can't make victory lane big enough for two teams and two cars, so somebody is always going to be disappointed,'" said Jarrett, who had already been looking for a sponsor to fund his own team in 1996. He actually had a contract from Hooters restaurants on his desk. The money was there, but Jarrett had a wife and two daughters, ages five and seven. The thought of taking them

with him to appearances at Hooters restaurants wasn't particularly appealing.

Jarrett didn't sign the deal, but he was facing a deadline. And then Yates had a change of heart. Irvan would be back late in the 1995 season and Yates decided that if he could field two cars for the rest of that year, he could do it for 1996 as well.

"I realized then and there that's why I hadn't signed that contract," Jarrett said. "There was going to be something there waiting for me. Everybody says God works in mysterious ways. You just don't know. Good things come to those who wait. I waited, and look what happened."

What happened was the birth of one of NASCAR's best teams.

CHAMPIONSHIP SEASON

With new crew chief Todd Parrott on board, Dale Jarrett won the Busch Clash and the Daytona 500 to open the 1996 season. He won the Coca-Cola 600 at Charlotte. He outdueled Ernie Irvan to win the Brickyard 400 at Indianapolis. Jarrett finished third in the points that year, then lost the 1997 championship by just 14 points to Jeff Gordon despite winning seven races. Jarrett won three more races and more than $4 million in 1998, but took a step back in the quest for a championship in a year that saw Gordon win 13 times, a modern-era NASCAR record.

At the end of the 1998 season the Yates team gathered for its annual holiday party. Jarrett handed out cards to each member of the team that read, "It's amazing what can be accomplished if no one cares who gets the credit."

From the day the 1998 season ended, Jarrett, Parrott, and Yates turned their team's focus toward winning the 1999 title. They talked about what they needed to change, about the new people they needed to hire, and about how they needed to approach the 1999 season with one goal.

"We didn't talk about doing those things to win races," Jarrett said. "Those were the things we needed to do to win the championship . . . We knew what we felt like had cost us the opportunity to win them."

The 1999 season was not perfect for Jarrett and his race team. He wrecked in the Daytona

500, rolling his No. 88 Ford over in a multicar crash that left him with a 37th-place finish. He battled back to second in the points before winning for the first time that year in May at Richmond, a win that moved him to the top of the standings. He won at Michigan in June, at Daytona in July, and at Indianapolis in August.

Just as important, as the season progressed he made the most out of days when things didn't go exactly right for his car and his team. After 22 races he had a 314-point lead and a championship within his reach. There were some hurdles left to clear—a crash in the race at Bristol and in qualifying at Darlington—but he clinched the title at Homestead in the

1999 NASCAR WINSTON CUP CHAMPION DALE JARRETT
ROBERT YATES RACING

season's next-to-last race and finished 201 points ahead of Terry Labonte, still driving for the Joe Gibbs Racing team that Jarrett had left before coming to Yates' team.

A week after turning 43, Jarrett went to New York to be crowned NASCAR's Winston Cup champion. He and Ned joined Lee and Richard Petty as the only father-son combinations to win their sport's top prize. And as Jarrett stood at the pinnacle, he couldn't help but reflect on the long, twisting road that had led him there.

"I don't know that I ever allowed myself to dream enough to think about winning a championship," he said. "Yes, I dreamed about winning races. . . . But I would have thought I would have had a better chance of jumping off of the Empire State Building and living than winning the championship.

"Take a look at where we all have been, what we came through and how we got there, and use that as inspiration that if you set out to do something, you can make it happen with hard work and dedication.

"You can do and be anything you want to in this country. Nobody is stopping you. You can work and work and accomplish it. The opportunity to do anything you want is out there, if it's playing sports or being a teacher or a doctor or a lawyer—whatever you want to do. You can do it. You just have to find what is right for you."

For Jarrett, there was still more to be done.

AN UNBELIEVABLE JOURNEY

Wt the start of the 2002 season Dale Jarrett was told that only 12 drivers had won races in NASCAR's top series after reaching their 45th birthday. Jarrett turned 45 in November 2001.

"I go back to Dale Earnhardt," Jarrett said. "He was still winning and very competitive and maybe on the verge of having another of his better years before he was taken from us."

Jarrett had won 20 races between ages 40 and 44, the same number that Earnhardt and David Pearson had won in that range. Only Bobby Allison (27) and Lee Petty (26) won more.

"Guys now are in better shape," said Jarrett, who started an extensive conditioning program after turning 40. "The competition also is closer, and that keeps your adrenaline going a little bit more. Hopefully we can change those statistics a little bit."

It took patience and perseverance, but in June 2002 Jarrett finally got it done.

He took advantage of teammate Ricky Rudd's bad break, a loose lug nut on a late pit stop, to take the lead in a race at Pocono and get his 29th career win, breaking a 30-race win-less streak.

"When you get in a little bit of a slump you honestly wonder when and if another win is going to come," said Jarrett, who'd had only two top-five finishes in his first 13 starts of the

Dale Jarrett

season. "But you sort of get a feeling when things are going to start to turn around.

"I told Kelley I thought I was going to win this race, but when I was sitting there in second behind Ricky I thought I was going to be wrong."

A few weeks later at Sonoma, California, Rudd got a victory of his own. In a season in which the sport's "young guns" were beginning to make their mark, the Robert Yates Racing teammates were showing they weren't ready to turn in their helmets quite yet.

In August at Michigan International Speedway, Jarrett made it 30 career victories by recovering from a spin through the infield grass on the 11th lap and going from fourth to first after a restart with 11 laps to go on four fresh tires. The victory came on August 18, 2002, the 11th anniversary of his first career win at the same track in the Wood Brothers' car in 1991.

Jarrett can look back now at all of those turning points in his career. The opportunity to drive for the Wood Brothers gave him the chance to get his first race victory. Going to the Gibbs team allowed him to see how hard it was to start a team from scratch as well as how rewarding it was to see that team taste success.

With Robert Yates Racing, he pressed on through the early adversity and grew along with his team and his sport before becoming its champion.

Twice, at least, he'd been on the verge of starting his own team. Today he believes that path not taken could have been the most critical decision he ever made.

"I fully see now that you can't do both jobs," Jarrett said. "You can't own the team and try to do the job as the driver too. There are too many responsibilities. It just can't happen any more. I have a hard time driving and doing all of the things that we have to do with all of the sponsors now."

Jarrett's current sponsor, United Parcel Service, has brought another element to his career. Jarrett has made some of the most talked about and most creative television commercials in stock-car racing history, working

with his father, with rock stars, and even with the Muppets on the ads imploring him to give up the No. 88 Ford in favor of racing the big brown trucks used by the parcel delivery service that now sponsors his team.

The fact is that Jarrett could go a long way toward filling up one of those big brown trucks by piling in all of the money that he has won in his 25 years of racing.

Remember that first race in 1977 at Hickory Motor Speedway? Jarrett collected $35 that night, and he still holds the envelope that pay came in.

Today, if he had a million envelopes containing $35, he'd still need more to hold all he's won in Winston Cup racing alone—in 2002, he topped the $37 million mark for his career.

Not bad for an old goat from Hickory Motor Speedway.

Dale Jarrett

RUSTY RACE

A MECHANICAL RACER

Veteran NASCAR competitor Rusty Wallace is among a dying breed of older drivers who take a hands-on approach to Winston Cup racing. The 46-year-old Missouri native admits that the knowledge he has gained through handling his cars has propelled him to superstar status.

Without question, Wallace is a throwback to some of the greatest drivers—like Richard Petty, David Pearson, Bobby Allison, and Cale Yarborough—in NASCAR history. Those legendary drivers always tended to their own cars; it wasn't unusual to see a guy like Pearson with a cigarette hanging out of his mouth while he was working underneath his car.

Wallace grew up watching those drivers achieve greatness and has closely followed their approach to racing. Even one of those retired greats admits that Wallace is, hands down, the best driver on the Winston Cup tour when it comes to knowing all the parts and pieces on his cars.

"Rusty is a mechanical racer," said Petty, the winner of seven Winston Cup championships and a record 200 victories. "He's worked on cars all his life and he understands what his car is doing and he wants to be involved. I sort of compare Rusty to

Bobby Allison because both those guys know so much about their cars [that] it can get to a point where sometimes people are afraid to work with them. Those guys on the crew just couldn't figure out what they were supposed to do."

With the recent invasion of technology into the sport of Winston Cup racing, Wallace's hands-on approach has almost become a hindrance, Petty said.

"If Rusty's car doesn't work well, most of the time it's his fault because he planned so much of what went into the car," Petty explained. "I think one of Rusty's problems has been the sport has gotten so technical that some of that stuff has gone by him. It probably confuses him because I know it confused me when I was driving. Now all they do is put a driver in the car and he tells the crew whether it's loose or tight and they will adjust it for him. With the technology in

this sport now, all the drivers need to do is be able to drive the car and not worry about things like shocks or springs."

While it's evident that the youth movement is a growing trend in Winston Cup racing, Wallace is a firm believer that his experience is the reason he remains one of the best in the business.

"I think the experienced drivers have always been on the top when all is said and done," Wallace explained. "The veterans always seem to rise to the top because they've been there and done that before. We understand what the tracks do throughout the course of the race and things like that. Racing is very different than stick-and-ball sports. Stick-and-ball sports are all about how strong you are, how fast you can run, how good you can catch the ball, and stuff like that. Our sport is more like, 'Man, I've been to this track 20 times and it does this same thing all the time.' The veterans tend to play off of that."

Wallace, though, will admit that it has been a challenge to adapt to the ever-evolving technology.

"The chassis setups nowadays in these cars are so hard to figure out it's incredible," Wallace said, "especially with the tires being as hard as they are now, and this super amount of down force on these cars. I think it really shows staying power to run 36 races and be able to be consistent each week. Remaining competitive has been what has kept me going."

Wallace has also admitted that it gets harder to win races when a driver reaches the age of 45. Only 72 drivers over that age have won a Winston Cup race. But for Wallace, racing is the only life he has ever known.

"This is what I do for a living," Wallace said. "NASCAR Winston Cup Series racing is what I've based my whole living off of, and I've enjoyed it a whole lot. I do look in the mirror occasionally and ask, 'Do I look old? I don't feel old. I don't think I look old.' I know I'm 46 and people think that's old, but I feel like I'm driving as well as I have in a long, long time. Not too long ago, I sat down and I asked my team owner, Roger Penske, to give me a straight answer about what he thought about my driving. Roger told me I'm driving as well as he has ever seen me drive since I've been with this team. I still feel really good behind the wheel. I feel like I'm still on top of my game."

IN THE BEGINNING

Knowing the intricacies of racing came early for Rusty Wallace thanks to his father, Russell Wallace, who was a three-time track champion in the St. Louis area. In addition to Rusty Wallace, brothers Kenny and Mike Wallace also shared a love of racing.

Rusty Wallace made his driving debut in 1973 at Lakehill Speedway in Valley Park, Missouri, and was named Rookie of the Year in the Central Racing Association. Between 1974 and 1978 Wallace caught the eye of many racing fans as he competed in more than 200 stock-car feature events.

Wallace joined the U.S. Auto Club circuit in 1979 and used five victories and a second-place

finish in the final points standings to win top rookie honors. In 1983 he won the championship in the American Speed Association in a series that has proven to be a great learning experience for young drivers looking to make it at the Winston Cup level.

"I ran the ASA circuit with guys like Mark Martin and Davey Allison," Wallace reflected. "All us guys grew up racing together."

Wallace impressed more than a few people in March of 1980 when he made his first career Winston Cup start at Atlanta and finished second behind Dale Earnhardt. Wallace made one more start that season, at Charlotte, and finished a respectable 14th. Over the next two years he ran only seven races with very limited

success, and he didn't run a single Winston Cup event in 1983.

Wallace came back full throttle in 1984 and won Winston Cup Rookie-of-the-Year honors, learning the ropes at NASCAR's top level with a pair of top-five finishes before ending up 14th in the final point standings. After posting two top fives in 1995, Wallace announced he was leaving team owner Cliff Stewart to join Raymond Beadle's Blue Max team.

The decision to move to Beadle's team in 1986 eventually paid huge dividends to Wallace and the No. 27 Pontiac camp. After five years of trying, Wallace scored his first victory at Bristol in his 72nd career start and backed that up with another short-track win at Martinsville before ending the season sixth in the final points race.

Getting better with experience, Wallace picked up two road-course victories in 1987 at Watkins Glen and Riverside en route to a career-best fifth-place finish in the Winston Cup championship race.

It was just the beginning of one of the sport's legends in the making. In 1988, despite six victories and two poles, Wallace was the

runner-up to champion Bill Elliott by a mere 24 points. He entered the season finale at Atlanta looking to cut into a 79-point lead, but if Elliott finished 18th or better—which he did —there was no way Wallace could overcome the deficit.

Wallace did all he could by leading the most laps and winning the race, but he came up heartbreakingly short of obtaining the 1988 crown.

"I did everything in my power," Wallace said afterward. "To come so close yet be so far away—I'm pretty dejected. Bill's a good friend of mine and I congratulated him like I promised I would."

Elliott graciously said that Wallace's day as champion would come: "Rusty will be in my position some day."

It turned out to be sooner rather than later.

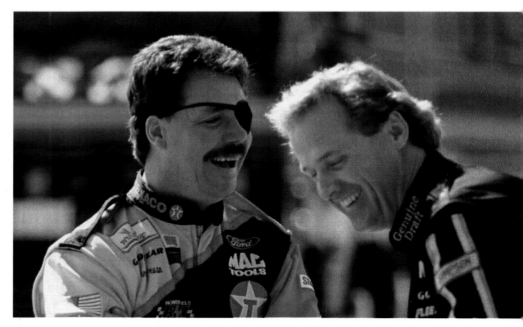

CROWNING MOMENT

After coming up short in the 1988 championship race, Rusty Wallace entered the 1989 season on a mission. It was a season in which the explosive growth of Winston Cup racing became even more evident; that year marked the first time that every event was televised live.

The timing couldn't have been better. With 10 races remaining, Wallace was in the thick of the title fight with Dale Earnhardt. The battles and heated rivalry between the two—who were the best of friends away from the track—were the stuff of legends. It was a rivalry that brought the fans to their feet whether the two men were racing for the lead or dead last.

The two competitors and friends also exchanged plenty of verbal jabs.

"I think both me and Rusty will run well," Earnhardt said. "We're pretty much in an equal situation. I'm going out there and run my own pace, and it's going to be a fast one. I'm not going to worry about the tracks or anyone else—especially Rusty. What he does is his business. I'm going to do what I want out there if I can."

Wallace countered: "I'm going to run my own race and I guess Dale will do the same. I'm not good at that psyching-out crap. Dale and I sort of have an agreement to where we don't stage anything phony. I'm going to run

hard every lap and lead all I can. All I want is the Winston Cup championship and I don't want anything standing in my way."

With five races remaining, the Winston Cup tour headed to Charlotte Motor Speedway. Earnhardt held a 75-point lead over Wallace. Thanks to a broken camshaft that ended Earnhardt's day only 13 laps into the race and the resulting 43rd-place finish for "The Intimidator," Wallace left Charlotte with a 35-point lead.

Two weeks later the Winston Cup Series headed to the now-defunct North Wilkesboro Speedway for a 400-mile shoot-out in the picturesque North Carolina foothills. It was a race that Earnhardt dominated, but it also ended up being one of the greatest finishes in NASCAR history.

As Earnhardt raced into the first turn, Ricky Rudd made a bold move to take the lead, and the two spun and wrecked as Geoff Bodine slipped by to steal the victory. Wallace was also a benefactor of the bizarre turn of events as he grabbed a seventh-place finish on the final lap and gained two more championship points over Earnhardt, whose battered mount limped to a tenth-place finish.

Earnhardt was livid over Rudd's actions, and a bitter rivalry developed between the two. "They ought to fine [him] and make him sit out the rest of the year," Earnhardt said.

Controversy would follow Earnhardt into the next race at Rockingham. This time Wallace was an active participant. As Earnhardt and Wallace were attempting to make up a lap they had lost during a green-flag series of pit stops, the two made contact and the famous black No. 3 came out on the short end of the deal. While Wallace was able to regain control of his Pontiac, Earnhardt's Chevrolet spun and was hit hard by Sterling Marlin's car. Wallace gained 72 points and led Earnhardt by 128 markers, with only two events remaining.

The next race was at Phoenix, and the verbal jabs were still going strong.

"We're going to Arizona for an Old West gunfight, but my team is taking a cannon," said Wallace, who had a mathematical shot at clinching the championship if major problems befell Earnhardt.

Wallace led the race early on until a tangle with Hollywood stuntman and racing journeyman Stanton Barrett sent the No. 27 Kodiak Pontiac into the second-turn wall. Wallace's car endured serious damage but managed a 16th-place finish while Earnhardt gained 30 points by ending up 6th.

All Wallace had to do at Atlanta was finish 18th and he would be the champion—but accomplishing that feat wasn't easy. Wallace struggled badly during the race, though he did manage to overcome a flat tire and two unscheduled pit stops.

"I said to myself, 'This can't be happening.' I thought the championship was slipping away," Wallace said. "It was scary."

It didn't help that Earnhardt dominated and won the race.

As he crossed the finish line, Wallace's crew radioed him some great news: his 15th-place finish was just enough to give him the 1989 Winston Cup championship by 12 points, the second-closest final margin in history.

"This wasn't the way I wanted to win, but it was all I could do," Wallace said. "We just hung in there. I don't care how sloppy it looked because this is the highlight of my career. I started dreaming about this as a kid back in Missouri, but I never thought it'd be a reality until I got with this team in 1986."

Earnhardt was gracious in defeat.

"I did what I said I was going to do," Earnhardt said. "I drove with all my heart. I didn't give the car a rest and it was prepared so well it stood the pace. I just wish I'd have been close enough in the points that Rusty would have had to race me for it."

90

THE NEXT STEP

After winning the Winston Cup title, Rusty Wallace won only two races in 1990—despite being in the hunt late in the season—but had three engine failures in the final four events to end the year sixth in final points. It also marked the demise of the once mighty Blue Max Racing operation, which closed its doors at the end of the season.

Not long afterward Wallace took advantage of one of the greatest opportunities of his career. Legendary motorsports mogul Roger Penske, who was looking to start a Winston Cup team, asked Wallace to take the ride for the 1991 season. Wallace accepted Penske's offer. The fledgling Penske South team won

only one race in its first season and finished 10th in the final championship race.

Wallace also won the 1991 International Race of Champions, a four-race series made up of the best drivers in the country from several different forms of motorsports.

Over the next two years Wallace dominated the sport by winning 23 races in only 58 starts. That equated to being victorious once in every three races. Despite the streak, Wallace and Penske would be the second-place team in 1993 and third in 1994—in spite of winning the most races both years.

The 1995 season was somewhat of a disappointment: the team earned only two victories.

While Wallace picked up the pace as far as victories in 1996, he failed to finish in six races. It was a year in which Wallace showed his driving diversity by winning on a short track, superspeedways, and a road course. Despite those victories, Wallace would end the 1996 season in seventh place in the Winston Cup championship race.

After turning 40 Wallace found victories and championships harder to come by. In 1997, he failed to finish a staggering 11 times out of 32 races. About the only bright spot of the season for Wallace was his lone victory at Martinsville. He ended that year ninth in the final points standings.

After enduring a season filled with mechanical failures that seemed to happen almost weekly, Wallace bounced back nicely in 1998. He picked up four poles, but for the second straight season Wallace could only manage one

victory throughout the year, at Richmond. He finished fourth in the championship race.

In 1999 Wallace again scored a single victory in the spring race at Bristol as fellow veteran driver Ricky Rudd failed to win a race for the first time in 16 years. Wallace became the only active driver to win at least one race per season, thanks to victories over 14 straight years. Wallace ended the 1999 season eighth in his bid for a second Winston Cup title.

After picking up a meager three wins over three years, Wallace and company returned to their usual winning form in a big way in 2000. In what he called one of the greatest victories of his career, Wallace won the spring race at Bristol to crack the elusive 50-win barrier and become only the 10th driver to reach that plateau.

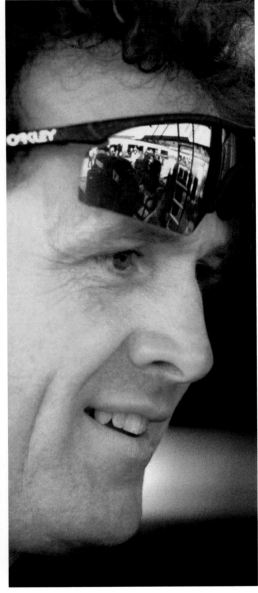

"Bristol has always been like a home track to me," Wallace said. "The fact that I won my first race there back in 1986 and my 50th win add up to making it a special place for me."

Before the 2000 season was over, Wallace picked up three more victories and finished seventh in the championship race. The victories allowed Wallace to extend his winning streak to a 15th straight season while his finish in the final standings marked the 14th time in 16 years that he finished in the top 10.

In the 2001 campaign Wallace won at California to tie Rudd's modern-era streak of at least one victory per season for 16 straight years. But that year will, unfortunately, always be remembered for the death of Dale Earnhardt, the seven-time Winston Cup champion. Wallace ended the season seventh in points for the second straight year.

WALLACE

ADAPTING TO CHANGE

In spite of the new technology now pervasive in his sport, Rusty Wallace still believes his past experience is a major part of his success.

"You're not going to be continuously successful on a race track unless you understand your car inside and out," Wallace said. "You can't just get out of the car and say, 'My car's not handling, so fix it for me.' I get out of my car and say, 'Change that spring, that shock, or sway bar.' I learned all that because I built my own cars. I painted my own cars and I hauled my own cars. I used to build my own engines, so I did everything when I was learning the sport. Because of that I became sort of a 'motor head.'

"So when my guys build me a good car at the shop and they build me a good motor to bring to the track, it's up to me to make it handle as well as possible. I'm the type of driver that got actively involved in that aspect of it and I'm glad I did that. Because if I didn't get involved, I would have had to rely on too many other people."

But in today's ever-growing evolution of technology in Winston Cup racing, Wallace has had to adapt. One thing that has been a tremendous asset to Wallace is the addition of

rookie sensation Ryan Newman as a teammate at Penske Racing in 2001. A graduate of Purdue University with a degree in engineering, Newman is yet another of the young drivers entering the Winston Cup Series with a nontraditional approach.

"Ryan has been real aggressive in his thought process," Wallace said. "I haven't been nearly as aggressive with some of the new things going on. Some of the new guys are running supersoft front springs. They're running tons of front sway bar and real gigantic rear springs and I'm like, 'Man, that's just too far off the beaten path for me.' If I tried that, I'd have big handling problems, and I didn't want to take that chance. I've kind of taken a conservative approach because I would have never thought that stuff would work. Now that I see it working, I'm more apt to get aggressive.

"It really has changed because you just can-not believe that what you never thought would work starts working. I've talked to Mark Martin, Jeff Burton, and Jeff Gordon, and even those guys can't believe this new stuff is working."

As the 2002 campaign wound down Wallace was without a victory, attempting to keep his winning streak alive at a record 17 straight years. Despite several near misses—including being bumped out of the lead with two laps to go at the Bristol night race by Gordon—Wallace badly wants to keep his streak intact.

Wallace has won 54 career Winston Cup races—second among all active drivers behind Gordon—but the 55th victory has proven to be very elusive.

"It's been grinding on my nerves and a tough thing to handle," Wallace said. "It's been

killing me because we've been so close. It's one thing if I'm running around towards the back of the field, but my cars have been awesome all year. I've got to close the deal now and get it done. It's getting deep into the year and I am a bit on the ragged nervous side, so to speak. I've won every year now for 16 years and I'd love to keep that winning streak going. If I don't win a race, it's going to be a sad day for me, I can promise you that."

Wallace understands the focus on the younger drivers coming into Winston Cup racing, but it bothers him to hear some say the veterans are no longer capable of getting the job done.

"I think everybody is sick of hearing all this 'young guns' stuff and all this veteran stuff," Wallace said. "We are all drivers trying to do the best we can do. Some people have hyped all that crap up and I'm sick of it. Thankfully it's tapered off a little bit."

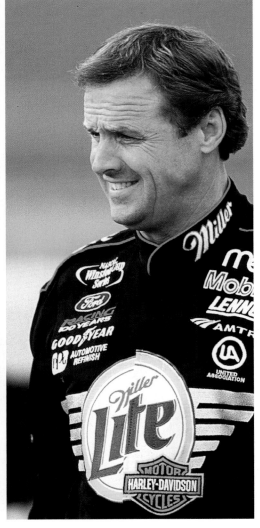

RICKY RUDD

TRUE GRIT

NASCAR Winston Cup driver Ricky Rudd is the personification of determination and consistency. Thanks to his ability to win races on a regular basis, the 46-year-old Rudd is one of the sport's living legends.

It seems fitting that Rudd heads into the 2003 Winston Cup season riding a NASCAR-record steak of 767 consecutive Winston Cup starts, a feat that has earned the Virginia native the nickname of "Iron Man." Though the focus has been on the sport's talented young drivers, Rudd is one veteran who should not be overlooked.

Entering his 27th full season of Winston Cup competition in 2003—and his first year with the legendary Wood Brothers Racing team—Rudd is one of only 72 drivers to have won a race at NASCAR's top level at the age of 45 or older. Rudd knows he's racing against the clock but still believes he can get the job done on any given Sunday.

According to fellow Winston Cup driver Jeff Burton, racing is very different from other sports, like basketball or football, whose over-40 athletes rarely remain competitive. The 35-year-old Burton believes that Winston Cup drivers only get better with age.

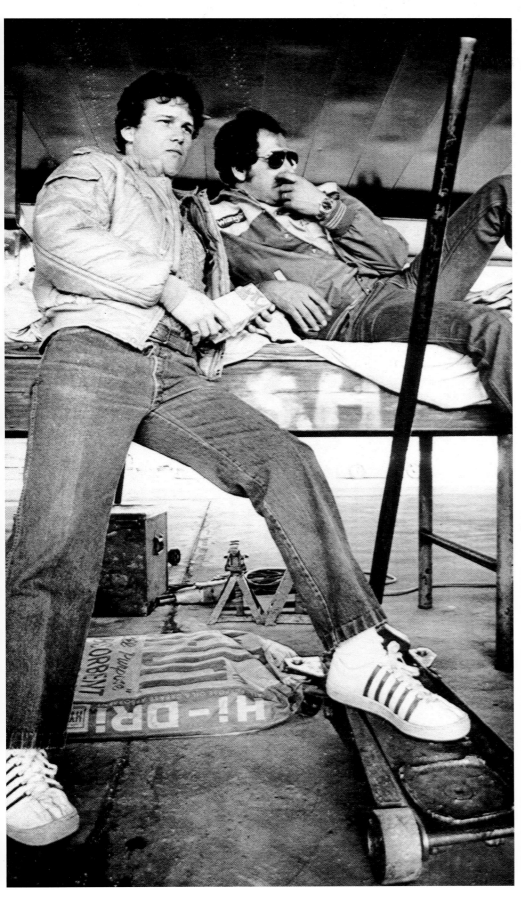

"It used to be that drivers entering Winston Cup did so at a much later age than those players coming into the NFL or the NBA," Burton said. "Experience matters in this sport because a driver's reaction time doesn't slow down the same way your legs slow down when you start reaching 45. There are things in racing that don't affect you as much compared to [what affects] a professional basketball player. They talk about Michael Jordan being old, but he can still do it. Well, he's not old in our sport because it isn't about how fast you can run up and down a court, it's about how well you can drive a car. It's two totally different things.

"From a physical standpoint, there's no reason a driver can't be successful as they get older. There are things that start happening to drivers from a psychological standpoint when they start to get older, I think, and maybe they're not willing to risk it all. But there's no reason, from a physical standpoint, that drivers can't continue to be successful past the age of 45."

Rudd agreed that experience is an advantage in the ever-changing world of Winston Cup racing.

"I think, if anything, it helps me to be a little smarter about things," said Rudd, who has 23 Winston Cup victories. "It was just a different time when I was coming up. I was 18 or 19 years old when I ran my first Winston Cup race.

In that time period, the next youngest guys, by the time they made it to the Winston Cup level, were in their early thirties. That was pretty common at the time. You really didn't have anybody who was a sure thing in their teens or early twenties at that time because they had to earn their way to Winston Cup. They had to run the Saturday night tracks and show promise and then eventually move up.

"As far as walking up to another driver and asking for help, they were more than helpful. I probably got most of my education by standing on top of the trucks and watching guys like Richard Petty, David Pearson, Buddy Baker, Cale Yarborough, and all those greats. I'd get on top of the truck and watch them drive off in the corner and watch when they ran out of gas. I just studied those guys a lot."

Since the sport has become so driven by technology, Rudd said, it doesn't take a num-

ber of years and past Winston Cup experience for a young driver to step into a top ride and have the chance to be successful.

"I've watched all these young guys come along and they have shown a lot of talent," Rudd said. "A lot of that can be attributed to the teams because you have to look at the equipment those guys are sitting in. Back in the old days, drivers came in here and had to earn those rides. Jeff Gordon sort of started this because he came in with very little experience and got into a Hendrick car with good equipment and experienced people. He did very well. I think that's what we're seeing today.

"Jeff Gordon is a good guy, but there are other guys with as much talent and they're jumping into these cars, with great people working on them, and obviously doing a good job. Is there any magic there? I think the magic is in the race teams themselves because they've got young drivers and experienced people working together. Sometimes it works and sometimes it doesn't."

After Gordon came along and made the most of his success, he was quickly followed by a host of other young and unproven drivers.

Tony Stewart displays an incredible amount of talent behind the wheel of whatever car he drives. Yet, in spite of his open-wheel racing roots, nobody could have fathomed that he would become the most successful rookie in NASCAR history by winning three races and finishing fourth in the final 1999 Winston Cup points standings. Dale Earnhardt Jr. and Matt

Kenseth came along as rookies the next season and both visited victory lane.

In 2001, rookie Kevin Harvick won two races during an emotional first year. He was thrust into the limelight after Dale Earnhardt's fatal, last-lap wreck in the Daytona 500.

With only four races remaining in the 2002 Winston Cup Series, it was very much a season in which the youth movement became evident. Rookie driver Jimmie Johnson led with three victories and was in competition with fellow first-year driver Ryan Newman, who had one victory. Remarkably, both were in contention for the Winston Cup championship. In addition to Johnson and Newman, sophomore driver Kurt Busch picked up three victories while Kenseth led the Winston Cup tour with four. Stewart led the points standings with less than a month left in the 2002 campaign.

Further illustrating Rudd's argument that it has become much easier for young drivers to win races is the story of Jamie McMurray, who won the 2002 fall race at Charlotte in only his second career Winston Cup start.

"There is no doubt about the fact that you've got some young guys who have come into this sport and done an excellent job. You can't fault them for that," Rudd said. "There have been a lot of young drivers to come along through the years, but probably not that many with the opportunity a lot of these young guys have got today. Certainly they've got the talent. There have been a lot of past young drivers that have come and gone because they didn't have the top-notch equipment. It's really about timing. First of all, good equipment is one thing, but you've got to be able to do something with that good equipment. If you don't, you probably won't get another year to prove yourself. These guys are proving themselves and doing well."

A VETERAN'S PERSPECTIVE

S ome of the veteran NASCAR Winston Cup drivers—including Ricky Rudd and Rusty Wallace—were somewhat resentful of the media's focus on the sport's young stars in 2002. They felt that their careers were being overlooked.

"You should give credit where credit is due," Rudd said. "If you're doing a good job and getting it done, whether you're young or old, it shouldn't matter because all these teams are motivated. Those are the guys that work really hard and put a lot of hours into these cars. If their car is up front, they deserve to be mentioned. If somebody is in the back of the pack, then you can understand people getting skipped over."

Probably one of the biggest reasons some of the veterans were perturbed about the focus on youth is their belief that the up-and-coming drivers have not worked as hard as their predecessors. Young drivers now earn millions of dollars early in their careers; their predecessors often made just enough to put food on the table.

"Go back 10 or 15 years and guys had to drive junk before they got a chance to get into a good car," Rudd said. "Even though they were driving junk, they got educated, and when they got to a good car they could appreciate it. The guys coming in today are stepping right into winning cars. All they have to do is learn how to drive the car. The car is there and they

adapt themselves to the car. Ten years ago it didn't happen that way. Nobody put a rookie—even one with the best ability in the world—in a Winston Cup car."

When Rudd and a lot of his fellow veteran drivers arrived on the scene, it took a lot of blood, sweat, tears, and sleepless nights to prevail in the sport. After years of racing, Wallace, Rudd, Dale Jarrett, Bill Elliott, Terry Labonte, and Mark Martin have reached superstar status.

Rudd's first season at NASCAR's top level was an impressive one. He drove for a team owned by his father, Al Rudd Jr. In 1977 he won top Winston Cup rookie honors and finished 17th in the final points standings after completing a 25-race schedule.

In 1978 Rudd and his father's team ran in only 13 events. In an 18-race schedule in 1979, Rudd started to turn heads by finishing ninth in the championship race while driving for legendary NASCAR team owner Junie Donlavey. Rudd once again ran 13 races for his dad in 1980, but got what proved to be a major break late in the season when he agreed to drive for team owner Bill Gardner in 1981.

"The early part of my career was such a struggle just to get from one race to the next," Rudd recalled. "In the early days we would run one race and then might have to skip five or six before we could get cars built back together and go race again. The early part of my career was always a struggle just to get with a team that could run all the races."

The move to Gardner's DieGard Racing team paid dividends after Rudd won three poles and finished second on three occasions.

By 1982 people had begun to notice young Ricky Rudd's talents. Another opportunity arose that year after Rudd moved to Richard Childress Racing to drive for the retired driver, who would go on to fame and glory as Dale Earnhardt's team owner.

"Ricky was a young guy that was determined to win," Childress said. "He was a young driver that didn't want to lose and he'd get mad when he lost. That fit the mold I was looking for."

While many race fans might think Earnhardt gave Childress his first victory, it was actually Rudd early in the 1983 season at the old Riverside road course.

"It was huge when we won at Riverside," Childress reflected. "It was Ricky's first win as

a driver and my first victory as a car owner." Rudd picked up another win later that year at Martinsville before ending the season with four poles and a ninth-place finish in the Winston Cup standings.

After leaving the Childress operation at the end of 1983, Rudd began a successful four-year stint at Bud Moore Engineering. Once again, Rudd was able to come into an established team and perform well under pressure. Over the course of his four seasons with the Moore team, Rudd won six races and never finished worse than seventh in the Winston Cup standings.

In 1988 Rudd continued what had become a trend of changing race teams on a somewhat regular basis when he moved to team owner Kenny Bernstein's King Racing team. They

enjoyed limited success, though, as Rudd won only one race during each of his two years with the team. He left at the end of the 1989 season, and later moved to Hendrick Motorsports to drive for Charlotte businessman Rick Hendrick. When Rudd joined forces with Hendrick, he was a teammate to former Winston Cup champion Darrell Waltrip and Ken Schrader.

The best season in the early part of Rudd's career came in his third year with Hendrick, when he finished second in the 1991 Winston Cup championship race to Dale Earnhardt, ending up 195 points in arrears.

In August of 1993 Rudd made what he said was one of the hardest decisions of his career: leaving Hendrick Motorsports to chase a life-long dream of owning his own race team.

When the Winston Cup tour rolled into Daytona Beach in 1994, Rudd had formed Rudd Performance Motorsports and acquired sponsorship from Tide. While almost everybody figured it would take a while for the new team to become competitive, Rudd proved those skeptics wrong with yet another victory and a fifth-place finish in the final standings.

Rudd remained strong in his second year as both an owner and a driver. In doing so he picked up what he calls his greatest victory, in August of 1994, when he won the Brickyard 400 at the famed Indianapolis Motor Speedway. Rudd picked up his second straight top-10 finish in the points in 1995, but had to wait until late in the season for a win at Phoenix that kept his streak of victories intact.

CHANCE TO SHINE

Ricky Rudd will be the first to admit that his 1996 and 1997 seasons left a lot to be desired. The strain of running the financial and competitive sides of his team was becoming almost impossible to bear. It also didn't help that a record number of multicar teams had made their way into the sport.

Rudd once again had to wait until late in the campaign during 1998 before he won at Rockingham in October. The on-track lack of performance was becoming more and more evident. Rudd's victory was his only top-five of the 1998 season. He finished 17th in the Winston Cup standings, his worst season in the final standings since 1979.

Unfortunately for Rudd, things didn't get any better in 1999, when he failed to win a race. That ended his winning streak and left him at a disappointing 31st place in the standings. In September he announced that he was selling his team to owner Robert Yates because he didn't have a sponsor lined up for the following season. He was asked to stay on board and drive the famous No. 28 Texaco Ford for Yates in 2000.

"I tried the ownership deal as long as I could without going to the poorhouse," Rudd explained. "I'm glad, looking back on it now, that a major sponsor didn't come along. It was hard when it came time to shut the team down

because of all the work it took to build it, but I couldn't have planned it any better."

For Rudd, returning to an established team—solely as a driver—revive his career. If he wrecked a car, he wouldn't have to spend part of his life's savings to replace it. The various bills that needed to be paid were no longer his problem. All Rudd was responsible for was getting into the car and trying to win races.

"After six years as an owner and driver, it was really nice just worrying about driving," Rudd said. "Doing both just got harder and harder because the Winston Cup schedule is so grueling. There just wasn't enough free time in a day. My days still got filled up, but not so much in the management role. I left the day-to-day headaches up to Robert Yates, and it was refreshing. It almost felt like I wasn't doing my job because I had a little more free time on my hands."

While many thought the pairing of the veteran driver with Yates might lead to a first title for Rudd in 2000, things didn't work out that way. Though in the hunt numerous times, Rudd was snakebitten by often-bizarre circumstances that kept him from winning. As a result Rudd went winless for the second straight season and finished fifth in the final Winston Cup standings.

Rudd proved his move to the Yates team was a smart one in 2001 when he enjoyed one of his best seasons in Winston Cup racing and clawed his way back into championship contention. In one of the most popular victories that season, Rudd snapped an 88-race winless streak when he drove the famed No. 28 to victory at Pocono in June.

"I'm not getting any younger," Rudd said afterward. "I don't have a tremendous amount of time left in my career and it was nice to get back to victory lane. I want to go out—when I do go out—with a bunch of wins."

True to his word, Rudd picked up a thrilling victory at Richmond over young Kevin Harvick a few weeks later. With the lead in hand and the laps winding to a close at the Virginia short track, Rudd was given what he called a "cheap shot" by Harvick, which knocked him from the

top spot. Moments later and with six laps to go, Rudd caught up to Harvick and repaid the favor with a "love tap" to grab the lead and claim his second victory of the 2001 season.

In fact Rudd—at age 45—was back in the thick of the Winston Cup championship race for the first time since his battle with Dale Earnhardt in 1991. Rudd's hopes were dashed, however, by two mechanical failures in August at Indianapolis and Michigan. Though once again coming up short of the championship, Rudd could take some comfort in having finished in the top 10 in final points for the 10th time in 18 years. He ended up with a respectable fourth-place finish.

The 2002 Winston Cup campaign took a strange twist for Rudd and his team following their June victory at the Sears Point road course. As the Winston Cup cars were testing

for the Brickyard 400 at Indianapolis, Rudd made it known that his return to the Yates team next year was doubtful. Rumors quickly surfaced that 2002 might be his last year of racing for Yates—or anyone else.

Rudd was also exploring whether to drive for team owner Chip Ganassi or the Wood Brothers. Many thought Rudd would take the Texaco sponsorship to a new Ganassi team. Turns out they were wrong. Rudd and Ganassi couldn't see eye-to-eye on several key issues and both began to explore other options.

"I just wanted to make the right choice and I didn't want to be pressured into making a hasty decision," Rudd said. "I wanted to kick the tires and look at all the teams inside and out."

THE FINAL COUNTDOWN

After more than a few sleepless nights, in late August of 2002 Ricky Rudd announced that he'd inked a lucrative three-year deal with the Wood Brothers beginning with the 2003 season. Rudd's move to the Wood Brothers was something of a tradeoff because the team's former driver, Elliott Sadler, switched to the Yates team.

Wood Brothers co-owner Eddie Wood said that after Sadler decided to move on he wasn't sure how the team would survive—until Ford and sponsor Motorcraft stepped in with additional funding.

"Elliott Sadler is where he wants to be, we got who we wanted, and Robert Yates got what

he wanted," Wood said. "We said from the beginning that until Ricky Rudd was signed, we were not going to sign anyone else. It was a dream and a hope that we would get him. There were times you didn't know whether it was going to work. You hoped it would, but then it would go away and come back, it would go away and come back. Fortunately it worked out for us all."

Rudd said it wasn't about money, but rather the chance to go to an established team that had a legitimate shot at winning races on a regular basis.

"I just don't have a lot of time left in this sport, so I didn't want to go to a team that was

in a building process and would need two or three years to really be competitive," Rudd said. "I've known the Wood Brothers a long time and know what they have done through history and what they can do in the future. I have watched them put competitive cars on the track each week for years. My first priority was to get with a race team that could win races right out of the box and challenge for a championship."

Rudd has been part of Winston Cup racing for a long time and has raced against some of the greatest drivers in history. He has seen two generations of drivers come and go. Rudd knows that he will eventually decide to retire

from Winston Cup racing. That decision will, undoubtedly, be one of the hardest he'll ever make.

"I look at it and in the back of my mind I've set a goal for myself that before I turn 50 years old, I won't be racing anymore," Rudd said. "I'll make it pretty close to the age of 50 and hopefully still have my health. I've got a wife [Linda] and a young son [Landon] at home, and I'm sure he would like to have his dad go and watch him play his baseball games and stuff. Right now I'm coming off one of the best years I've had in my career driving, contended

for the championship most of the year, and went to victory lane.

"But somewhere along the line—if you race until you're 60 or 70 years old—the performance is going to start falling off. I'm just taking it a year at a time and as long as my abilities haven't deteriorated, I'll be out here another year. It could be a year or it could be two or three years, but it won't be longer than five."

If there's one thing Rudd is very proud of, it's being in the Coca-Cola 600 in May 2002 at Charlotte, when he surpassed the record of fellow veteran Terry Labonte by making his NASCAR-record 656th consecutive start without missing a single race.

"It shows determination and obviously a lot of dedication," Rudd said. "But it's just come naturally. I don't feel like I've done anything that most other guys wouldn't have done. Maybe a couple of times I probably drove with injuries that some other drivers might have sat out that weekend. This is all I've done since 1981, getting in the car and giving 120 percent, whether it was for my team or somebody else's team."

Rudd believes that, because young drivers now appear to dominate the sport, the days of drivers racing late in their careers might be numbered.

"I don't see myself or somebody like Dale Jarrett here in another five or six years," Rudd

said. "I don't see a third of the garage area here in another five years. I think you're going to see guys continue to come in much younger, but leave much younger. It will probably sort of mirror the Formula One circuit, where those younger guys come in at like 30 years old and then move on. I think you're going to see that trend probably start to happen. It's already started."

IRON AND ICE

Terry Labonte has a racing resume that few can match. Others have won more races or claimed more championships, but Labonte is the only active NASCAR driver to have won all of the following:

- Winston Cup Series championship (twice)

- International Race of Champions title

- The Winston All-Star race (twice)

- Busch Clash (now the Budweiser Shootout) at Daytona

- Winston Cup races on tracks of one-half mile, three-quarter mile, one mile, 1.5 miles, 2.5 miles, and road courses

- Endurance races at Sebring and Daytona Beach, Florida

He even has more than one nickname. Some prefer "Iceman," a tag he earned on the Texas short tracks for his unflappable style behind the wheel. Others like "Ironman," a moniker given Labonte for starting in 655 consecutive races. The streak began January 14, 1979, and ended August 5, 2000. Labonte even drove silver race cars to mark milestones along that record-setting path, including his 514th straight start on April 1996 to break Richard Petty's record, and his 600th consecutive race in October 1998 at Phoenix, Arizona.

Labonte entered the 2002 season with 709 career starts among active drivers. He trailed only Dave Marcis (881) and Ricky Rudd (731).

"Seven hundred is a lot of races, a lot of years," Labonte said. "It really doesn't seem like it's been that long since I first showed up at Darlington. The time's gone by pretty fast, but I still enjoy doing this."

Since his first NASCAR race in 1978, Labonte has built a career that puts him in an elite class of drivers. Entering the 2002 season—Labonte's 25th in NASCAR—his achievements have become legendary: two championships, 21 wins, 26 pole positions, a NASCAR record of 655 consecutive starts, and more than $26 million in winnings. Along the way, the Iceman or Ironman has been involved in many of stock-car racing's finest hours:

- Until Jeff Gordon's title in 1995, Labonte was the youngest Winston Cup champion of the modern era (post-1971), winning the 1984 title at age 27 years, 11 months.

- Terry and his brother, Bobby, are the only brothers to win Winston Cup championships in NASCAR history. Terry won in 1984 and 1996, with Bobby winning in 2000.

- Labonte won the 1989 International Race of Champions (IROC) title, one of six IROC series in which he has competed. The series matches drivers from different motorsports in identically prepared cars in an attempt to have the drivers' skill—not the equipment—determine the outcome. Labonte's 1989 championship included a victory at Michigan Speedway. He even clinched the 1993 IROC title for the late Davey Allison, through his substitute effort in the final event at Michigan in August of that year.

- Labonte is one of eight Winston Cup drivers who qualified at a speed in excess of 210 miles per hour in May 1987 at Talladega, Alabama, prior to NASCAR's restrictor-plate era.

- With his fourth-place finish in the 1982 Old Dominion 500 at Martinsville, Virginia, Labonte became the youngest driver in motorsports history to win $1

million, and the 12th NASCAR driver to reach the mark.

- With his 1996 NASCAR championship, Labonte became the fifth driver to win multiple titles in the sport's modern era (post-1971), joining Petty and Dale Earnhardt (seven each), and Cale Yarborough and Darrel Waltrip (three apiece). Jeff Gordon, Labonte's Hendrick Motorsports teammate, has since joined that group with four titles, including back-to-back championships in 1997 and 1998. In 53 years of NASCAR Grand National Division and Winston Cup Series competition, Labonte is one of 13 multiple titlists—a list that includes Buck Baker, Tim Flock, Ned Jarrett, David Pearson,

Lee Petty, Herb Thomas, and Joe Weatherly.

- Labonte's victory in The Winston in 1999 was his second triumph in the annual winners-only special event and came exactly 11 years to the day—May 22, 1988—since his first victory. In addition, Labonte has finished second once (1987) and third twice (1985, 1997).

Fans might be surprised to learn that none of those achievements rank as Labonte's personal favorite. In fact, he says it was an event that didn't even occur on the track.

In September 2001 at Dover, Delaware, Labonte started his 700th race. Three days later he and his brother, Bobby, were

honored in their hometown of Corpus Christi, Texas, as the only brothers to win NASCAR Winston Cup Series championships. The city renamed one of its public parks Labonte Park.

"In more than 20 years of racing, that was the proudest moment I've had," Terry Labonte said of the park dedication. "It goes beyond wins, poles, championships, prize money, and other racing records. I grew up there, and to have a city park dedicated in your name is truly one of the highest honors any citizen can receive.

"I will forever be grateful to the city and am very appreciative of the special day that was planned for my family," he said. "I am so very proud to call Corpus Christi my hometown."

IN THE BEGINNING

When Terry Labonte was growing up in the coastal city of Corpus Christi, Texas, he had two lofty dreams.

The first was to drive race cars on NASCAR's big-time Winston Cup circuit. The goal wasn't all that farfetched, for Labonte had proven his courage and touch for driving a car at a young age, winning the national quarter-midget championship when he was 10.

September 4, 1978, was the date of Labonte's first NASCAR race, the Southern 500—one of the sport's most storied and prestigious events. Starting 19th and finishing 4th in the No. 92 Duck Industries Chevrolet of Hagan Racing, Labonte won $9,800. At the

time, not many racing fans knew the kid from Corpus Christi.

Brought to Winston Cup racing by team owner Billy Hagan, who had sponsored Labonte's cars at a Houston short track, the youngster gained some attention with that Southern 500 debut on one of NASCAR's most unforgiving tracks.

"I didn't realize all the tradition at Darlington and how tricky the place is," Labonte said. "I'll never forget going into the mandatory rookie meeting and they showed a video.

"In the film the car I was going to drive, No. 92, had made the highlight of all the crashes during the previous race at

Darlington. I sat there and cringed every time I saw the car on TV.

"I said to myself, 'Whatever you do, don't go out there and make next year's highlight film.' I just tried to stay out of trouble."

Labonte did, finishing only a lap behind three of the sport's greats, Cale Yarborough, Darrell Waltrip, and Richard Petty.

Labonte competed for Hagan Racing in 12 of his 24 Winston Cup seasons (1978–1986 and 1991–1993). He left the team based in Thomasville, North Carolina, to race for Junior Johnson & Associates (1987–1989).

Labonte earned his first victory in his 59th start, the Southern 500 at Darlington on September 1, 1980. He won his first pole position in 1981, earning the number one starting spot for the spring race in Atlanta.

As a child, Labonte's other dream had been to climb into the cockpit of the machines fielded by the legendary Johnson of Wilkes County, North Carolina. Labonte achieved that second dream, driving for the Budweiser-backed No. 11 Chevrolet team. Johnson's highly respected team, led by crew chief Jeff Hammond, who is now an NBC commentator, fielded cars out of a sprawling shop in picturesque Ingles Hollow in the foothills of the Brushy Mountains.

Labonte succeeded Darrell Waltrip with the Johnson team. At the time Labonte joined Johnson, his cars had accounted for 75 triumphs and six titles over the previous 10 seasons, far more than anyone else.

"Junior has the best ride in NASCAR, and the figures back it up," Labonte said. "I couldn't be happier. But I wouldn't have accepted Junior's ride if I didn't feel I could get the job done. And that job is to win as many Winston Cup championships as we can."

Labonte admitted the pairing seemed unlikely at the time.

"In the nine years I've been in Winston Cup racing, I doubt that me and Junior ever said 10 words to each other before we teamed," he said. "To be honest, I thought he was just some sort of figurehead. Boy, was I wrong! When I got over to his team, I found out he knows everything. Engines. Chassis. Team morale. Junior Johnson does a whole lot more than lean on a jack or a race car."

Of Labonte, Johnson said: "We wanted a driver who was intelligently aggressive, and Terry fits that description perfectly. At first glance, when we started making plans to replace Darrell, a lot of drivers looked attractive. But after studying [them] we saw that some of them failed to meet the standards we've set for ourselves and didn't perform consistently.

"Terry meets the standards, and I think one of the things he is best known for is his consistency."

Johnson didn't know that Labonte's consistency would lead to a NASCAR record. And at the time, Labonte felt he was at the sport's pinnacle.

Although the dream pairing didn't produce a championship for Labonte, it did provide some memorable wins. In 1988 Labonte ran away with The Winston All-Star stock car race at Charlotte (now Lowe's) Motor Speedway. He became the fourth different champion in as many runnings of the special event race, joining Waltrip, Bill Elliott, and Dale Earnhardt as a winner of the sport's richest single purse, $200,000. It was Labonte's biggest payday to date and a victory he called the most important triumph of his career.

In July 1989 Labonte, who had been beaten four times at Talladega Superspeedway, finally made it his turn to finish first at NASCAR's fastest track.

Labonte, driving a Ford, held off Waltrip and his potent Chevrolet in a dramatic dash covering the final five laps to win the event by about a half-car length.

Labonte had been a runner-up three times and a third-place finisher once at the 2.66-mile track.

"I'd rather win here than any place I've been because I've come so close so many times," Labonte said after the victory. "It's just a great win for us."

The outcome extended Ford's Winston Cup winning streak to five straight. Labonte started it in June at Pocono (Pennsylvania) Raceway with his first win of the 1989 season. It was also the fourth victory with owner Junior Johnson, whose cars hadn't triumphed at Talladega since Waltrip swept both Talladega races for him in 1982.

Labonte would leave Johnson's team to form his own in 1990, then joined Hendrick Motorsports in 1994. Labonte marveled at how much the sport had changed.

"I know when I ran my first race in Darlington I set the car up myself and drove the truck down there," he said. "Most guys don't have to do that today. But that's how [it was] years ago when everybody was starting out; that's how most people started out. There weren't the big teams. There were only a few top teams that won the races and had the established drivers and everybody else was kind of in the same boat. Things have changed. It's just different today than it was then."

IRONMAN STREAK

Terry Labonte's streak began on January 14, 1979, at Riverside Raceway in California, a road course that no longer exists. He was 22 at the time and had run only five Winston Cup races, including the Darlington race, in fall 1978.

"I wouldn't have imagined ever running so many in a row," Labonte said. "When I started my career, this is probably the one record that I never would have thought about.

"I didn't start thinking about it until a couple years ago and people started bringing it up. It seemed like an impossible thing to do."

Through consecutive starts, Labonte experienced a few streak-threatening calls.

"I've had to take a few provisionals through the years," he said. "It's kind of funny. Somebody brought up the fact that, [for] a couple of cars I drove, the biggest accomplishment was just making the races in them."

Labonte won the 1984 Winston Cup championship with Billy Hagan's team, posting two victories, 17 top-five finishes, and 24 top-10 finishes.

Without a doubt, Labonte's Ironman streak would have come to an end where it began—at Riverside—in 1982, except for

one thing. The race there in November was the season finale.

Labonte was involved in a horrifying single-car crash that left him with fractures of the foot, leg, ribs, and nose. He had deep lacerations about the face.

"That crash at Riverside really hurt," said Labonte, who went airborne at the end of a long straightway and barrel-rolled into the infield. "It's the worst I've ever been injured," he said. "There's no way I could have raced again anytime soon, but I had almost three months to mend before we ran again, so I was ready to go at the start of the '83 season."

There were rumors that Labonte, while lying in a Riverside hospital bed, was in so much pain that he decided to quit racing.

"If I had thought that would make me feel better, yeah, I would have done it," Labonte said. "If you burn your hand in a fire, you don't want to put the hand in the fire the next day.

"I thought, 'I don't know. . . . That was a pretty bad wreck.' But after a while I got to feeling a little better, didn't dwell on it anymore, and picked up and went on."

In 1996 Labonte eclipsed NASCAR's "King" Richard Petty for consecutive starts.

"To break Richard Petty's record . . . I mean he *is* stock-car racing," Labonte said. "It's an honor for me to be mentioned in the same paragraph with him, much less be able to break one of his records."

In recognition of the occasion, Labonte was asked to throw out the first pitch before a Baltimore Orioles–Boston Red Sox baseball game April 16 at Camden Yards in Baltimore. He met baseball's "Ironman," Cal Ripken Jr., and posed for a photo with him that was placed on a card for collectors.

By 1996 Labonte had gone four years without a victory in one stretch. Three years earlier, Rick Hendrick had called and asked him to join Hendrick Motorsports.

During the season, an "expert" picked Labonte to win the title over his teammate, Jeff Gordon, the 1995 champion.

"I'd pick Terry as far as understanding how to win," the expert said. "He won one championship, back in '84, and he knows what it takes. He's lost enough over those years between and he's hungry. I think he's deserving."

The expert? Seven-time champion Dale Earnhardt.

In November 1996 the season finale featured three drivers with a chance at the title:

Labonte, Gordon, and Dale Jarrett. It might have been Labonte's most memorable day on the track.

Knowing what was at stake that Sunday, Labonte didn't leave anything to chance. When Gordon developed tire trouble that put him two laps down before the race was 10 laps old, Labonte streaked to the front to assure himself of the five bonus points that come with leading a race.

Hendrick was like a nervous father in the pits, worrying over Gordon's and Labonte's teams as the race played out. Halfway through the race, he "took enough aspirin to kill a normal person," then finally breathed a sigh of relief after winning a second straight championship.

Knowing a finish of eighth or better would clinch the championship, Terry backed off at times during the latter stages, steering clear of lapped traffic. In front of him,

Bobby was putting the finishing touches on an ideal end to the season.

"We're a little different than some brothers in racing; we actually like each other," Terry Labonte said. "That was pretty special today—it really was."

With a golden November sunset as a backdrop, brothers Bobby and Terry Labonte shared each other's glory late that Sunday afternoon at Atlanta Motor Speedway.

When both victories were secured, the brothers drove side-by-side on a victory lap unlike any other.

"That [dual victory lap] is something I'll cherish forever. It's the coolest thing we've ever done," Bobby Labonte said as fireworks exploded in the sky behind him.

For a Texas family that moved to North Carolina in the late seventies so

the boys could pursue their love of racing, it was a nearly perfect day. It was so good that Terry, racing's Iceman, was brought to tears.

While Bobby ended the season with a .41-second victory over Jarrett in the NAPA 500, Terry's fifth-place finish secured the Winston Cup points championship. He earned his second championship trophy, this time with the No. 5 Kellogg's Chevrolet.

"This was a really big day," he said after beating defending-champion Gordon by 37 points for the $1.5 million prize. Jarrett finished third in the points race, 89 behind the champion.

Labonte's regular-season winnings of $1.9 million for 1996 were almost three times the amount he collected, including bonus money, for the entire 1984 championship season.

Twelve years after winning his first Winston Cup championship, Labonte took prerace painkilling shots to numb the pain from a broken bone in his left hand, then snuffed out any hopes Gordon and Jarrett had of overtaking him in the points battle.

"This is something I've worked a long time for," Terry said afterward. "It meant a lot to win it again after winning it 12 years ago. The first time I won it, I thought, 'This is neat. Maybe I'll do it again next year.' I didn't think next year would ever get here."

Labonte's "Iron Man" streak of 655 consecutive starts was broken August 5, 2000, when he missed the Brickyard 400 at Indianapolis while recovering from injuries suffered a month earlier in a race at Daytona Beach, Florida. It was Richard Petty's record of 513 straight starts that Labonte broke in 1996, just as Ricky Rudd surpassed Labonte's mark of 655 in 2002.

Labonte, feeling the lingering effects from wrecks in back-to-back races in July, chose not to drive in the Brickyard 400 at Indianapolis after he felt dizzy on his first lap around the track that morning.

"I noticed it when I got down into Turn 3," Labonte said. "I really had a hard time focusing. It was kind of strange. You go 200 mph at this place

and you've got to be right. I know there are some people who've run, and I am probably guilty of it, too, but you can't do it, you shouldn't do it. I didn't feel like I needed to be out there."

Labonte suffered a concussion and a broken bone in his right leg in a crash during the Pepsi 400 at Daytona on July 1, then was involved in another crash in the New England 300 the following week at New Hampshire International Speedway.

Despite ending the streak, Labonte's 700-plus total starts amazed his brother, Bobby.

"Seven hundred starts are a lot of races and we're not talking about 700 starts on a short track, running 35 or 40 laps every Saturday night," Bobby Labonte said. "This is 400, 500, and sometimes 600 miles at a time, so it's quite an honor, and I'm proud of Terry for what he's accomplished."

TANGLING WITH EARNHARDT

Even though the 1996 championship finale was memorable for Labonte, fans might put a race that Labonte didn't win at the top of the list.

In August 1999 Labonte led on the last lap at the Saturday night race, but a nudge from Dale Earnhardt sent the Kellogg's Chevy into the wall at Bristol Motor Speedway and left Labonte steaming.

On a night when NASCAR had been particularly punitive when it came to driver infractions, the inaction on the Earnhardt-Labonte incident was conspicuous.

On Lap 99, for example, Jerry Nadeau was penalized two laps for "aggressive driving" after hitting points leader Dale Jarrett's already damaged car.

On Lap 411 Dave Marcis was docked one lap for "intentionally causing a caution" because NASCAR felt he stopped on the track despite having ample opportunity to get to pit road. The implication was that Marcis was trying to get a yellow flag so Earnhardt—whose car owner, Richard Childress, often provided Marcis with support for his racing—could pit under caution.

But without definitive evidence that he intentionally wrecked Labonte, Earnhardt kept his 73rd victory and fans got a controversy.

The obvious irony is that a controversial ending to an Earnhardt victory was the kind of thing Winston Cup fans lived for. The finish fueled arguments among fans for weeks, and it certainly

didn't hurt ticket sales for future races at Bristol. It's part of the reason promoters fill more than 140,000 seats around a half mile of concrete.

"Race fans are great people," said Earnhardt, who heard boos in victory lane. "They're great critics, too. If they're not cheering, they'd better be booing me. I've got big shoulders, and I can take the blame or the pressure or whatever. I'm sure we'll hear about the race for awhile, and we'll just have to take it like it is.

"I have to take what comes and race from here on," Earnhardt added. "Was I not supposed to try to pass him back? I know I wasn't supposed to try to wreck him, but was I not supposed to try to get back to him and get under him?"

Labonte didn't start any fights that night—that would have gone against his "Iceman" demeanor—but he did sound a warning.

"He'd better tighten his belts up," Labonte said of Earnhardt.

Earnhardt knew Labonte wouldn't be his best buddy.

"We'll have to wait and see if he punches me out or won't talk to me or just waits until the next race or whatever," Earnhardt said. "Terry is a great racer. We've raced a lot over the years. We went hunting and have done some things together, but you know, people get upset. I can apologize to him all day long and that's not going to change what happened."

Three years after that controversial race, Labonte remains dedicated to returning to victory lane and contending for another championship.

"I tell you what, once you've won races and once you've won championships, there's not a better feeling than when you leave Sunday afternoon and you've come back and you've won the race or you had a great run, and been competitive and had a shot to win the race," he said. "I

think just the desire to be back on top again, the desire to win that next race again, to win that next championship, that's what it's all about.

"That's what we work for. It's a very tough accomplishment to win the championship. That's what drives me, anyway, the desire to win another championship, a desire to win the race this weekend or next weekend or the Winston or whatever. That's what keeps you going."

With NASCAR racing becoming much more of a national sport than a Southern phenomenon, the focus is always on the next hot young driver. While Labonte believes the so-called "young guns" have tremendous talent, he knows they're getting opportunities to prove themselves early in their careers.

"The biggest difference today is you see young drivers that come in that really have an opportunity to be with top-notch teams right from the start," he said. "Normally, years ago, when rookies would come in they would be with teams that aren't on top of the list as far as the equipment and everything else like that. Things are a lot different today. . . ."

With the equipment and talent at Hendrick Motorsports, Labonte says all the ingredients for another title run are on board.

"If we get this team back the way it needs to be, there's no doubt in my mind that we can win another championship and win races," Labonte said. "We've got the people and we have all the pieces. Now we just have to put them together. I want to be back in the points race so bad, and the key to that is consistency. First you have to start running in the top 10. Then you work on top fives, and if you can do that, the wins will come."